FINAL CHOICES

SEEKING THE GOOD DEATH

Michael Vitez

Photographs by
April Saul and Ron Cortes

Camino Books, Inc.
Philadelphia

Manufactured in the United States of America

1 2 3 4 5 00 99 98

Library of Congress Cataloging-in-Publication Data

Vitez, Michael.
    Final choices : seeking the good death / Michael Vitez.
        p.   cm.
    Includes bibliographical references and index.
    ISBN 0-940159-43-0 (alk. paper)
    1. Death—Social aspects—United States. 2. Death—Moral and
ethical aspects—United States. 3. Terminal care—United States.
4. Medical ethics—United States. I. Title.
HQ1073.5.U6V57   1997
306.9—dc21   97-33714

Cover and interior design: Robert LeBrun
Cover illustration: Beth Starkey

For information write:
Camino Books, Inc.
P.O. Box 59026
Philadelphia, PA 19102

For Mom and Dad

CONTENTS

ACKNOWLEDGMENTS

This book would never have been written were it not for Max King, editor of the *Philadelphia Inquirer*, where the material first appeared. He sensed tremendous reader interest in end-of-life issues, and he challenged me to write something with more sweep, impact and heart than anything I had ever done. I am indebted to Max for his vision and support.

I also want to thank my editors, Donald Drake and Dotty Brown. There is no greater support for a writer than to know he's working with superb editors whose judgment he can trust, who can take a good story and make it great. The highest compliment I can pay them is that their fingerprints are invisible.

So many others should be thanked. I am grateful to all the subjects of these stories, for they trusted me—a stranger—to enter their lives at such an emotional and chaotic moment. These people were often heroic, always gracious, and I hope this book proves worthy of their trust.

The photographers—April Saul and Ron Cortes—captured the most tender moments. Their talent is humbling.

I also want to thank my wife, Maureen, and our three kids for their support and patience during the reporting and writing. Rather than a marathon, it was a dead sprint for seven months. My wife shared the exhilaration, the heartbreak, the exhaustion with me day after day. I could not have done it without her understanding.

Michael Vitez

INTRODUCTION

What should we do about dying?

The question may seem odd, silly, even naive. We all know that each and every one of us will die, and so wondering what to do about it seems on a par with wondering what we should do about gravity, or the fact that triangles have three sides. Dying is inevitable, a reality of our world. We do not 'do' anything about it. We can choose what attitude we want to adopt toward death—stoic, frightened or even hopeful, but we cannot do anything about it.

When the question is raised what you or I should do about death, what is really being asked is, can anything be done to take the mystery out of dying? There are plenty of books and a considerable number of television programs and movies devoted to the demystification of death.

This demystification can take the mainstream form, exploring the metaphysical significance of our mortality or biological theories about why living things die. Or efforts to take the mystery out of death can push the envelope all the way out to the fringe, where one finds books that purport to explore the nature of death through understanding near-death experiences or television programs that feature channelers and psychics claiming to be in contact with those who are dead.

None of this works, either. Despite humanity's best and most noble efforts, as well as its goofiest and downright screwy theorists and theories, the mystery still clings to death. We cannot know on the basis of our reason what, if anything, awaits us after we die. We can wish, have faith, even feel convinced about what will happen when we die, but wishes, faith and feelings are clear proof that death remains firmly wrapped in mystery.

Even if you eat fiber every morning, swallow an aspirin every evening, sleep under a pyramid every night and jog three miles a day, you still cannot do anything about your mortality. True, you can buy yourself some time but the Grim Reaper will still visit no matter how many sit-ups you do.

To concede ultimate victory to death is not to concede the legitimacy of the question of what we should do about dying. The fascinating cases presented in this book show that the practical issue facing modern medicine and politicians in this and other nations is not death but dying. While we have no power over whether we will die, we can have some control over how, when and where we will die.

We can die alone or among those who know us. We can die in pain or demand that vigorous efforts be made to minimize our suffering. We can die in a hospital, a nursing home, a hospice or a home. We can die full of tubes or die without any medical assistance whatsoever.

The problem with dying is that the way we now manage it, in our hospitals and our long-term care facilities, it is all too often a nightmare. Too many people die with pain. Too many die with treatment being administered that they do not want. Too many people die in a hospital because the support their families would need to take them home to die is not there. Too many people go broke dying.

In fact, the situation surrounding dying in America is so bad that there are many who believe that suicide or assisted suicide is far preferable to the fate that currently may await them.

Can dying be made more humane? Certainly. More conversation and more care will go a long way toward this end. So will settings that are more familiar and spiritual and emotional support that is aimed at the person rather than the person's disease. Aggressive pain and palliative control are also obvious steps that must be taken to get us down the road to a better death.

Those who want to make dying better could not do better than to carefully listen to the voices of patients and families who have experienced dying as it now is in the American hospital. By meeting the people Mike Vitez writes about in the pages that follow, little will happen to make death less of a mystery but much can be learned about how to solve the mystery of making dying more humane and dignified.

Arthur Caplan
Center for Bioethics
University of Pennsylvania

1 Learning how and when to let go

PATRICIA MOORE READ A POEM to her husband in the intensive-care unit. She stood beside him wearing a surgical gown, holding the dog-eared book in her latex gloves.

Through her surgical mask came the tender, muffled words of "Knee-deep in June" by James Whitcomb Riley:

> *Orchard's where I'd ruther be—*
> *Needn't fence it in fer me!*

Gene Moore lay before her, unconscious. An IV line entered a vein in his neck and ran through his heart, into the pulmonary artery. It measured blood flow and carried five medicines into his infected body. A ventilator tube ran like a garden hose down his throat. A feeding tube pushed through his nose and into his stomach.

Bags on his legs inflated and deflated every few minutes to prevent clotting. A catheter drained urine from his bladder. He wore orthotic boots to keep his feet bent so

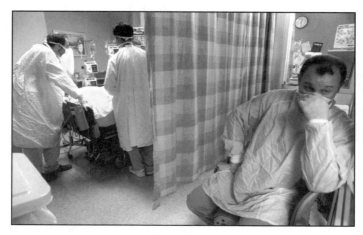

Terry Moore keeps vigil near the bedside of his father, Gene Moore, in intensive care at the University of Pennsylvania Medical Center. As doctors fought to save Mr. Moore, 63, family members were tormented by his suffering. They were pained, too, by the question of how long to let it continue.

that, should he ever, miraculously, get out of bed, this retired 63-year-old steelworker would be able to stand.

Mrs. Moore stood beside her husband of 44 years, her heart aching with indecision. Were she and her two sons doing the right thing putting him through this torture? Or should they stop? Should they tell the doctors to let him die?

MEDICINE HAS GOTTEN so good at keeping people alive that Americans increasingly must decide how and when they will die. They must choose if death will come in a hospital room with beeping machines and blinking monitors or if it will come at home, with hospice workers blunting the fear and pain that so often accompany the final hours. And soon, they may have a remarkable choice: Will they kill themselves with their doctor's help?

Americans are demanding options because they are beginning to care as much about the quality of their death as the length of their life. They want control at the end. They want a humane death, a good death.

Throughout the country, in hospitals and medical schools and court-rooms and statehouses, reformers are pushing hard to improve the way Americans die. Already, they have won the right for families to turn off ven-tilators, hold back life-sustaining drugs, and even take out feeding tubes.

Nearly 400,000 Americans every year now seek a tranquil death through hospice. Since 1982, when Medicare began covering hospice care, the cost has grown to $2 billion a year. Six years ago, the world had not heard of Jack Kevorkian. Yet in 1996 two federal appeals courts ruled that patients have a right to assisted suicide. Those decisions were overturned in June 1997 by the U.S. Supreme Court, which referred the debate back to the state legislatures.

With this quest for control have come difficult ethical, social and person-al decisions that Americans are only beginning to wrestle with. Individuals and their families are approaching the end of life in different ways.

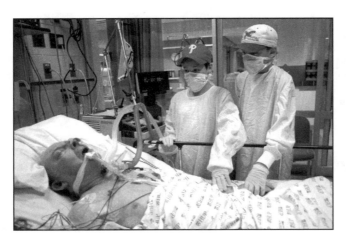

Mark (left) and Adam Moore visit Gene Moore in the intensive-care unit at Penn. They were poker-playing buddies of their granddad's.

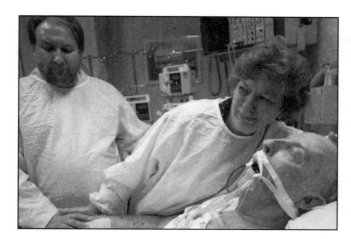

Patricia Moore, with her son, Ron, weeps as Gene Moore, her husband of 44 years, lies dying. "He's a fighter," Mrs. Moore said. The fight required a ventilator, a feeding tube, and an IV line carrying medicines.

The intensive-care unit offers a hope for recovery, but the price can be a miserable death. Deciding when to surrender can be a torture all its own.

Thousands of Americans find themselves in the same position as Mrs. Moore, standing beside a loved one, in intensive care, wondering what's happening, wondering what's the right thing to do.

FOR 24 YEARS, Gene Moore had lived in an 18th-century farmhouse in rural Ottsville in Upper Bucks County, Pa. From his back porch, he watched the sun set over endless hills. He grew grapes and made wine, shoed horses, and played classical guitar and poker with his grandsons. Every summer he'd go crabbing with the family in Ocean City, Md., and pour on the bay seasoning.

He dreamed of buying an RV and roaming the country with his wife and younger son, Ron, 35, who still lived at home. But then his lungs went bad—pulmonary fibrosis. By January, Gene Moore couldn't breathe. Then came the lung transplant in February at the University of Pennsylvania Medical Center. A step from death, he was reborn.

He regained enough stamina to walk two miles a day on his treadmill and went to a flea market where he showed strangers the scar—shaped like bat wings—that streaked across his chest. "One hundred and twenty staples," he would tell them proudly. He bought a 1981 Thunderbird, a life-long dream, and drove it twice before he found himself back in the hospital in late June. His body had rejected the lungs.

On July 7, 1996, Gene Moore was wheeled into Penn's medical intensive-care unit—the MICU. He was being kept alive by mechanical ventilator, feeding tube, blood transfusions, blood pressure medicines, steroids, antibiotics. He was heavily sedated.

Like many Americans, the Moores believed doctors could save almost anyone, cure almost anything. They had experienced one miracle, the transplant, and expected another. Death was inconceivable. But so was the agony of the intensive-care unit—until they lived it.

THE MOMENT Mrs. Moore walked through the big double doors into the ninth-floor intensive-care unit, she entered a world like no other, a world in which she was a complete stranger. Death was so near, the language of doctors so foreign.

The intensive-care unit consisted of 12 large rooms, wrapped around a busy nurses' station. Inside each room lay an extremely sick patient surrounded by a confusing array of pumps and monitors incessantly beeping. A solemn-faced visitor often sat at the bedside. Doctors, nurses went in and out. They were busy, on the move.

Gene Moore landed in 979, a corner room with a large window facing the nurses' station. Because of the risk of infection, everyone had to put on a gown, gloves and mask to enter his room and take them off on leaving. Mrs. Moore usually sat in a chair next to her husband's bed, waiting for a good word from a doctor. Something, anything, to sustain her, to give her hope. Perhaps his creatinine level was up, or some other obscure measurement she didn't understand.

Mr. Moore didn't have a living will—a legal document stating his preferences for end-of-life treatment—because he thought, incorrectly, that a will would take the decision-making out of his wife's hands and give it to the doctors. Mrs. Moore and Ron believed they would be in control.

"We are his living will," she said. But Mrs. Moore didn't understand what was happening, even though the doctors and nurses were very pleasant and answered all her questions. "I just don't know what to ask," she said. How could she decide what was best?

"You just don't know how far, how much to let him go through," Mrs. Moore said. "He has been to hell and back. He's had so many blood tests. His arms are so scarred they can't even get a needle in."

So she sat, hour after hour, day after day, beside her husband. He lay there, unresponsive, somewhere between life and death, while she passed the time doing the most ordinary things: reading him poems, planning vacations, mulling recipes for baked lobster Savannah. She wanted to believe he would return home again, soon. After all, almost 80 percent of the 700 or so patients treated in Penn's medical intensive-care unit each year leave alive, so why not her husband?

MANY REFORMERS BELIEVE that doctors and hospitals still focus too much on curing and not enough on caring for people at the end.

The largest clinical study ever of the sick and dying (10,000 patients, five hospitals, eight years) reported in 1995 that more than a third of terminally ill hospital patients died in pain. Many spent their last hours isolated from their families, their wishes about withdrawing life support ignored by doctors. Patient-doctor communication in the last days of life was poor, according to the $28 million study, funded by the Robert Wood Johnson Foundation in Princeton, N.J.

"We withdraw care when it's too late, when death is certain, when even the janitor knows," said Joan Teno of the Center to Improve Care of the Dying at George Washington University, a lead researcher in the study, which ended in 1994.

Advocates for change believe doctors are too optimistic, too sparing in what they tell patients. They say that families would be more willing to accept death earlier if doctors were more honest, more realistic.

Doctors at Penn's medical intensive-care unit say they are aggressive at withdrawing care—making the decision that further efforts would be futile and recommending to the family that the patient be allowed to die as comfortably as possible. They say the families don't want them to quit.

"Almost invariably families want us to push on when we want to stop," said Dave Gaieski, a resident doctor on the intensive-care unit. "It's only one in 20 that a family comes to us and says stop," said Cheryl Maguire, an intensive-care unit nurse for 10 years. "It's much more the case that we see there's no hope, and we keep working until they get to that point, too."

Ronald Collman, one of two attending doctors on the MICU and the man ultimately responsible for Gene Moore's care, knew that the odds were against him. But some patients like Moore survived. Collman thought Moore had a chance, and he knew the family wanted to fight. Collman said he believed intensive-care unit doctors give patients the ending they want.

"I think most of our patients die with dignity," Collman said. "We've confused death with dignity with a romantic death. Death usually is not

Patricia Moore thanks attending physician Ronald Collman. His priority at the end, he said, was to lessen her husband's pain.

beautiful. It's ugly. Death with dignity is death that's right for them. I don't mean futile things, but fighting and really giving them a chance. Patients are here because their family chose an aggressive fight. To die after an aggressive fight is an honorable thing, appropriate for that person."

MRS. MOORE MADE A FRIEND—Mary Lou Stephano, the wife of the comatose cancer patient in the next room. The Stephanos had met as students on the Penn campus 40 years earlier, in Houston Hall, across the street from the hospital.

Mrs. Stephano also expected her husband, Stephen, 62, to wake up and enjoy life again—at least for another year. Mrs. Stephano looked forward every morning to talking with Mrs. Moore in the lounge. Better than even Mrs. Stephano's children, Pat Moore understood what she was going through.

On Friday afternoon, July 19, 1996, doctors requested a meeting with Mrs. Stephano and her family. They scheduled it for Sunday. Mrs. Stephano told Mrs. Moore she thought the meeting was to update the family on how her husband was progressing. She was impressed by how considerate the doctors were.

Nurse Maguire knew that doctors didn't have much hope that Mr. Stephano would recover, and she wanted, gently, to alter Mrs. Stephano's expectations. Maguire told her that after three weeks in the MICU her husband would face a very long recovery.

Sunday morning, a few hours before the meeting, Mrs. Stephano asked the resident a blunt question: "Is he going to wake up?" She expected him to say, "Of course." The resident took a long time to answer. "A 15-to-20 percent chance," he told her. Mrs. Stephano was stunned.

During the hour-long meeting, the news only got worse.

Cynthia Robinson, an attending doctor working with Collman on the intensive-care unit in July, called the meeting. Attending doctors decide when it's time to recommend withdrawal, when to call a family meeting. Resident doctors say some attending doctors on the intensive-care unit have a reputation for keeping patients going as long as possible, while others recommend withdrawing life support much sooner.

Whenever Robinson or Collman held a family meeting, at least a couple of residents or interns sat in. What they learned was a vital part of their medical education: how to help families let go.

Robinson brought the Stephano family up to date. She was pleasant, thorough and compassionate. But she was also clear: If Mr. Stephano didn't improve within a week, she would suggest withdrawing life support. "Keep him comfortable," the doctor said, "and let the inevitable happen."

One son and a daughter-in-law sobbed quietly, crumpling tissues into piles on the conference table.

"If he could participate in this discussion here," the doctor asked, "what would he want?"

"We never had a chance to talk about it," Mrs. Stephano said. "But he lived for his mind."

Robinson left the family members to talk among themselves. After some discussion, the family concurred with Robinson.

As they walked back to Mr. Stephano's room, Mrs. Moore could see their faces, their tears, as they passed by. Now she knew what the meeting was really about.

MRS. MOORE AND RON always tried to arrive by 9:30 a.m., in time for staff rounds. Not that they understood much, but they might pick up something. On Wednesday morning, July 24, they found Collman and a bevy of younger doctors clustered outside Mr. Moore's room.

Paul McGovern, the resident in charge of Mr. Moore's day-to-day care, was giving his usual technical talk. The Moores stood off to the side and listened.

"Good bowel sounds . . . hypernatremic . . . positive 2 liters over last 24 hours . . . his wedge went up initially, BP 130/70 . . . white blood count was point 6."

"Oooooh," flinched Collman. "What was his chest film?"

"Worse," said Joe Schellenberg, another doctor. "Significantly worse."

After more discussion, McGovern concluded, "The plan here is pretty much the same, changing his lines over, begin weaning. . . ."

Mrs. Moore looked through the window at her husband and saw blood in his urine bag.

After the medical report, Collman walked over to Ron and his mother, as the residents, interns, medical and pharmacy students stood by quietly. When families are around, they get quiet. "He's had some backward steps," Collman said, looking into Mrs. Moore's soft, green eyes, which welled with tears behind the mask. "His white count is down, most likely one of the drugs we're giving him."

She pointed to the bag with the bloody urine. "Probably from the low platelets," he said reassuringly. "Not something to worry about."

"His X-ray is looking worse," Collman said. "The remarkable thing is his lungs are functioning well. It doesn't make sense; they look so bad, yet are functioning well."

Mr. Moore wasn't improving. And the dangerously low white blood-cell count signaled another crisis, this time for his bone marrow. Collman knew the odds of recovery were getting slimmer with each passing day in the intensive-care unit.

"We should all get together, in the next few days, and talk about what's happening," he said to Mrs. Moore and Ron, "just so we're all on the same page."

Mrs. Moore let go a long sigh. Ron reached out and held his mother, hugged her, then held her hand. "Doesn't sound good," he said. "No, it's not good," she agreed.

The Moores slowly, sadly, began to put on their masks, gowns and gloves. "He's a fighter," Mrs. Moore said quietly. "But I don't think he'd like this. What do you think, Ron?"

"He'd hate this," Ron said. "He'd hate it."

THE NEXT DAY, 43-year-old Terry Moore, the elder son, visited his father. Terry is a fundamentalist minister, pastor of Victorious Christian Church in Marlton, N.J. He believes in the word of God. He believes that everything possible should be done to sustain a human life.

Taking his hand, Terry spoke to his unconscious father with a preacher's conviction. "You're doing fine," he said. "Everything is going good. You're doing all right. BP's good, heartbeat is good, Dad. They're giving you some food, too, Dad. So you have every reason to be encouraged. We love you. And Jesus loves you most of all. He's right here by your side. He's got the situation right under control. . . ."

Terry Moore shared none of his mother's reservations. He told a story about his wife's grandmother in Northeast Philadelphia. She had a stroke. "They were all getting ready to shovel dirt on her," he said. "They were withdrawing things from her, and I said, 'What are you doing? She's not dead yet.'" The grandmother recovered.

"We believe in God," Terry Moore said. "We believe in prayer. We believe in miracles. So as long as there is life, there is hope."

BY FRIDAY, JULY 26, Mr. Moore had a new neighbor, two doors down. Rose Kennedy, 75, had had a stroke getting ready for church that week. In the intensive-care unit, Mrs. Kennedy was put on a ventilator. But the morning following her stroke, her family found her living will in a dining room drawer.

"If to a reasonable degree of medical certainty my condition is hopeless. . . can't recognize people or communicate . . . , I do not want my life prolonged. I do not want mechanical ventilation. . . ."

The family members agonized over what to do.

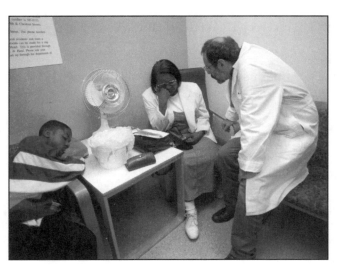

Ronald Collman talks with Betty Pryor about her mother, Rose Kennedy. Mrs. Kennedy's living will declared that she wanted no mechanical ventilation or artificial feeding. Kennedy's great-grandson, Antwain Wynn, rests nearby.

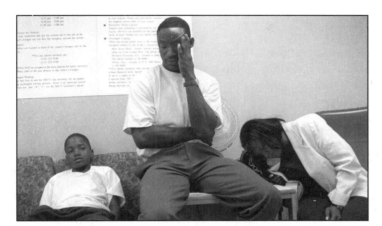

Rose Kennedy's son Wendell and daughter Betty Pryor wait for word about her condition with her great-grandson, Antwain Wynn. "It's just so hard to make a decision," said Pryor, who was designated by Mrs. Kennedy's living will to act in her behalf.

Wendell Kennedy and Betty Pryor at their mother's side in intensive care. Kennedy and the family knew Rose Kennedy's chances were grim. Mrs. Kennedy, 75, had had a stroke while getting ready for church. The next day her living will turned up in a dining room drawer.

Collman gathered them in the conference room. He said Mrs. Kennedy wasn't in pain and might recover some function in the next few days as swelling in the brain diminished. He urged them to delay a decision.

"Her paper says no tube and no vent," insisted Betty Pryor, her daughter and the person Mrs. Kennedy had designated as her proxy.

"I agree, that's what the paper says," Collman said. But he thought she might improve. "She's going to have brain damage. Not enough that she'll be a vegetable. But the difficult question is how much brain damage would be acceptable to her."

"When she filled out this paper, she didn't tell me anything," the daughter said. "That's why she's on the ventilator now." The daughter was crying. "It's just so hard to make a decision. So many ifs, buts."

"Her condition is not really covered in the will," Collman said.

Betty read aloud the key sentence: I do not want mechanical respiration, no artificial nourishment.

Collman was quick to respond. "When somebody says no artificial ventilation, we never had a chance to ask her about four days of artificial ventilation. We see a lot of strokes. From our point of view, that's not an extreme amount of time."

"Betty, let's give her two more days and see," said one of Rose Kennedy's sisters.

"OK," whispered the daughter, crying. "I'm just trying to do what she asked me to do. . . ."

Two days later, when Collman said it was unlikely Mrs. Kennedy would improve, the family chose to remove all life support. Mrs. Kennedy died peacefully a day later, her family at her bedside, soft jazz playing in the background.

ON SATURDAY, Mr. Moore was worse than ever. Even though he was sedated, he was so agitated. To his wife it seemed as if he were trying to wake up and talk, to scream. And his kidneys were starting to fail, a complication of his many medicines.

About 3:30 p.m., Paul McGovern, the resident, talked about Mr. Moore in the doctors' conference room. "He's losing all his cell lines," McGovern said. "Reds, whites and platelets. He's transfusion-dependent right now."

He elaborated on the medical dilemma that Mr. Moore had become. The treatments were wreaking their own havoc: One anti-infection drug was damaging his blood cells; another impaired his kidneys; infection-fighting steroids further decimated his immune system. And so on.

"We're doing more harm than good," McGovern said. "My personal belief is that we probably let these people go on longer than they should."

CARING FOR EXTREMELY SICK PEOPLE is expensive. The average daily cost at Penn's medical intensive-care unit is $1,575. America has 78,000

A LIVING WILL is a legal document that allows a person to accept or refuse end-of-life medical care. Some wills are detailed, others more broad.

Living wills have become increasingly popular since 1990, when Congress required hospitals and nursing homes to provide information to patients about living wills upon admission. Living wills were never intended to be used in emergencies, but rather as a guide. Advocates strongly believe that a living will alone is not enough, that families should talk among themselves well before a crisis arises about how much care and treatment an individual would want.

A medical power of attorney is a legal document that allows a person to appoint someone he trusts to be his spokesperson when he can't speak for himself.

For information on a living will, or for answers to other end-of-life questions, contact Choice in Dying, 200 Varick St., New York, N.Y. 10014, telephone 800-989-9455, fax, 212-366-5337.

For additional sources of information, go online to: http://www.phillynews.com

intensive-care beds, and the cost of caring for patients in those beds has been estimated at 28 percent of all hospital costs.

Reformers want to make sure that patients get the care they need, but not unnecessary or unwanted treatment. The key to humane and cost-effective intensive care is to treat those who will benefit, but not squander precious resources and impose futile treatments on those who will not. But often it is impossible to know who will live and who won't.

Ronald Collman says America wants to offer the most advanced technology and treatments to everyone, yet keep health-care costs down. How to balance those desires, Collman said, "is a discussion nobody wants to have."

LATER THAT SATURDAY AFTERNOON, nurse Lorrie Bokelman went into Mr. Moore's room to turn him, a routine procedure. As she turned him, Mr. Moore stopped breathing and became so agitated that the nurse pulled the curtain shut, leaving Mrs. Moore on the other side. The nurse began to "bag" him, forcing oxygen into his lungs manually. The curtain, a pretty plaid, fluttered as Mrs. Moore sat in her chair, next to a trash can for old bandages and used gloves, worrying.

She had heard the alarms and beeps, and seen that curtain close so many times, yet it never became easier. Mrs. Moore folded her face into her hands.

"Is he still kind of out of it?" she asked hopefully.

"Yeah," said Bokelman. "He just tried to hold his breath while we turned him. He looked like a beet for a second." Bokelman pulled back the curtain.

Mrs. Moore walked to her husband's side; she took his hand, stroked his head, spoke so softly that her words were nearly music. "How you doing, love? Just breathe, slow and easy, slow and easy, babe. It's all right."

ON SUNDAY, JULY 28, Mrs. Moore took a recreational vehicle guide to read. But before she and Ron could gown up, Collman and McGovern called them into the family room.

Mr. Moore's blood pressure was plunging. He appeared more agitated than ever. Already that morning, doctors had suctioned "coffee grounds"—dried blood—out of his stomach. They also found something alarming on his chest X-ray. Collman wanted a family meeting.

Mrs. Moore called Terry, then she and Ron collapsed in a corner of the hallway by the waiting rooms, sobbing in each other's arms. Even though Mrs. Moore had seen so much, had endured so much, 21 days in the intensive-care unit, this news devastated her. Until this point, no doctor had suggested she give up hope. She still had reservations the following month for their favorite apartment in Ocean City, Md.

Collman assigned Mr. Moore a new status: Do Not Resuscitate: Level B. This meant that no additional treatment of any kind, no more blood or antibiotics would be given. But life-sustaining care—the ventilator, the blood pressure medicine—would continue. At least until the family meeting. Nurse Bokelman injected Moore with a significant dose of an anesthetic to relax him.

When Mrs. Moore gathered herself and walked back into her husband's room, he was resting more easily than he had in a week. "Ohhhhh, that's better," she said with relief.

When Terry Moore arrived shortly after noon, the family gathered in the family lounge. "Your dad has been through a series of complications, and with each complication are new complications," Collman said to Terry. "We gave him a full course of treatment. The bottom line is that he overall has gotten much worse. . . . The blood counts are worse. He's fevery again. Lungs are worse. And he's had a real deterioration today. The big picture is the situation has progressed to the point where, in my medical opinion, there is no way we're turning this around. What worries me today is he seems much more uncomfortable. Lorrie's worked very hard to keep him comfortable. What I think we're doing is giving him treatments just to give treatments. They're not helping him. They're not prolonging his life."

Collman continued: "I think we should make absolutely certain he has as much pain medication as possible, even if that means the blood pressure gets lower, because keeping him comfortable is most important. I recommend we wean him off all the medications he's on, except for pain and sedation. I think it's likely if we stop the blood pressure medicine, he won't last very long."

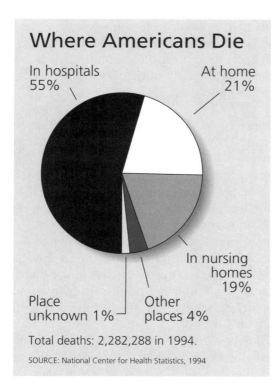

Where Americans Die

In hospitals 55%

At home 21%

In nursing homes 19%

Place unknown 1%

Other places 4%

Total deaths: 2,282,288 in 1994.

SOURCE: National Center for Health Statistics, 1994

Terry recounted the miraculous recovery of his wife's grandmother. Terry was polite but direct. "I don't want your mind-set—whether you're pro-abortion or whatever—to affect your decision," he said to Collman. "Have we maxed out on every technological thing—not just to keep him going—but to bring about a recovery?"

Collman responded softly and looked right in Terry's eyes. Mrs. Moore held her son's hand. "I believe we have not missed anything that could possibly help him recover. I'm even afraid we have possibly gone too far. We're at the point now, there is no chance of making him better. And I'm afraid we're making him suffer."

Collman asked the family to talk about it and let him know their decision. He shook their hands, thanked them, and left the room.

"Daddy was a fighter, all the way to the end," Mrs. Moore said. "But we have to let him go. Things are overwhelming."

"You make the decision, Mom," said Terry. "I'm satisfied they've done as much as they could do. It's in the hands of God."

Mrs. Moore went to find Mrs. Stephano. She needed someone who understood how she felt. Doctors had removed all life support from Mr. Stephano two days before and moved him to the step-down unit, down the hall from the intensive-care unit, to spend his last days or hours.

Mr. Stephano's room was empty. He had died the night before.

BY 4 P.M., THE HARD DECISIONS had all been made. Gene Moore was peaceful. His family was resigned to his death. Bokelman inconspicuously reduced the blood pressure medicine. She turned off all the alarms and beeps—no more mechanical distractions.

The family surrounded Gene Moore. They whispered their final farewells. Mrs. Moore rested her head against his chest. "Love you a whole bunch, sweetie pie. I love you so much. Here's Ron, your bowling buddy, holding your bowling hand. Just relax," she said to him softly, almost singing. "Just relax."

By 4:45, he had no blood pressure, but the heart kept fighting. Finally, at 5:15, Gene Moore's heart stopped.

Terry walked out and scribbled on his father's medical chart: "Homeward bound to see Jesus."

FOUR DAYS LATER, on Thursday afternoon, Ron and Terry went to a Quakertown funeral home and returned home with a cardboard box filled with their father's ashes. Mrs. Moore was surprised at how much the box weighed—four or five pounds.

Just as Gene Moore had wanted, the family gathered in a wooded area of their property. In front of a tall pine, on the side of a hill, Mrs. Moore sprinkled the ashes of the man she married at 16. Terry said a prayer. They opened a bottle of champagne and drank from plastic champagne glasses.

SIX WEEKS LATER, Mrs. Moore still couldn't write thank-you notes to those who had sent flowers and cards. "I just can't get started," she said. "I can't get back to living again." Every day she relived the days in the intensive-care unit.

"I have to conjure up all those awful things in order to say it was the right thing to do," she said. "I have to think of all the bad things to justify why we let him go."

Ron said, in retrospect, that he would have withdrawn care much sooner. Yet Mrs. Moore said she would do it all over again. She would fight until the doctors gave up hope.

EPILOGUE: In early November, Mrs. Moore had lunch at Mrs. Stephano's house. They were joined by another woman they met on the intensive-care unit whose mother had died after a long fight. "We all had red noses and went through many tissues," Mrs. Moore said, "but it was very cathartic. It was wonderful."

2 Going home to die, with hospice care to help

MARYANNE LOHREY DROVE UP FRANKFORD AVENUE in her 14-year-old Ford Granada, windows down, lost in thought. Everywhere she went now, she saw the houses of the dead—that house and that house and that house.

Each house and street and neighborhood conjured up a story, each one different, but also the same, the story of a death, an ending.

Mostly, those were not painful recollections but joyful ones, because this woman who made great lemon bars and drove an un-air-conditioned clunker had helped hundreds of people die. She was sure she had supported the families and helped the patients accept death and prepare for it, and, in the best cases, die well.

Lohrey was a social worker for the hospice program of Pennsylvania Hospital in Philadelphia. In May 1996, she was on her way to Kensington and a new patient, Steven Jacobs. All she knew was that he was 40 years old,

Steven Jacobs is comforted by his son, Steven Hendricks, 22, at their Kensington home. When it was certain he would not recover from a rare cancer, Mr. Jacobs told his doctor, "I just want to go home and rest until the time comes."

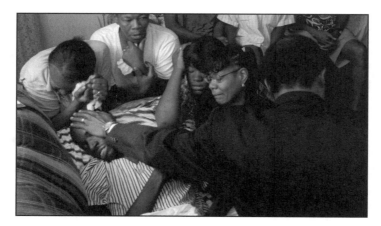

The Rev. James Luckey, a hospice counselor, prays with Steven Jacobs, dying of a rare cancer. With him were (from left) Linda; a sister, Nadine; his daughter, Gretchen, and a sister, Olivia.

had a family, and was dying from a nasal cancer that had spread to his lungs and liver.

She followed the directions, finally pulling onto a narrow, one-block street of cramped rowhouses. Crack dealers worked each end. She parked in the middle of the block and walked up to the front steps wondering: How could she and her colleagues help this man die?

She knocked on the door.

HOSPICE WILL HELP nearly 400,000 Americans die this year—almost one out of every six deaths.

There are 2,700 hospice organizations nationally, nearly 50 in the Philadelphia area. Medicare spent nothing on hospice until 1982. In 1995, it spent $2 billion.

This growth in hospice care is a reaction to the way many Americans have died in the last 30 years: in pain and feeling neglected by doctors; often in hospitals, attached to machines, suspended in a modern medical purgatory.

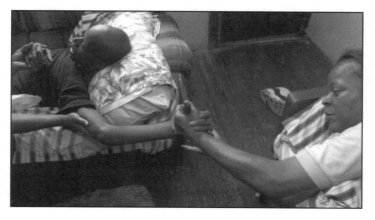

Steven Jacobs clasps hands with Linda Hendricks, his companion of many years. At the end, he made peace with regret at not having married her.

"We have created on some level this illusion that we can keep people alive," said John J. Mahoney, president of the National Hospice Organization in Washington. "In some respects, we can keep them alive. But what we've really done is just kept alive their suffering."

Hospice is a push forward, but into the past, an attempt to let people die the old-fashioned way—at home, surrounded by the things and the people they love. Hospice provides medications, medical equipment, nursing care, counseling, pastoral care, and even help with routine responsibilities, from cooking to laundry.

Growing numbers of Americans are choosing hospice, Mahoney said, because they want a humane death, a good death, a death on their own terms.

WHEN MARYANNE KNOCKED, Steven Jacobs' daughter, Gretchen Hendricks, answered the door. She was 19, just days away from delivering her second child. She had no idea who Maryanne was or what she was doing there. Maryanne asked to speak with Gretchen's mother and stepped inside.

The living room was dark and cool. Baby pictures hung on the walls, along with a portrait of the Rev. Dr. Martin Luther King Jr. and the words "I Have a Dream." A cat, Books, stretched out on the wooden floor.

Maryanne climbed the stairs to Steven's bedroom and found an emaciated man lying in a bed. Once 220 pounds, Steven now weighed 120. His head was shaved. His voice was slow, a little slurred, weak. "I know all about you," he said.

Steven Jacobs had worked hard all his life, for the last 10 years monitoring alarm systems for PNC Bank branches. He graduated from Bartram High in Philadelphia and served in the Marines. He believed in God and wondered what he had done—or not done—to deserve this fate.

In the bedroom with Steven were Linda Hendricks, whom Steven had dated since he was 15, and their son, Steven Hendricks, 22. Young Steven lived at home and worked as a certified nurse's aide in a nursing home. With them were two of Maryanne's colleagues who had arrived earlier— nurses John Sapovits and Nancy Juergens. Maryanne invited Gretchen to join them for this initial meeting.

"No!" Steven Jacobs insisted, waving Gretchen away. She was confused and hurt by the rejection, and already Maryanne could see she had work to do.

After Gretchen left, Steven explained that he hadn't told her that he was dying. "I didn't want to tell her because she is pregnant," he said. "She's not ready to know. . . . Ain't nothing heavier than this."

Maryanne and the others described the services that hospice would provide—social workers, nurses, pastoral counseling, even someone to cook and clean, if needed. Steven signed a do-not-resuscitate order. Hospice requires that the patient know that death is imminent and not fight it.

As Steven put pen to paper, Linda collapsed in tears. "You may know it up here," Steven said, pointing to his head, "but signing your name to a form, facing it, that's a whole other thing."

STEVEN JACOBS DIDN'T WANT to die. He saw himself as a provider and a protector, a man with many responsibilities still unmet. And he loved life too much to leave it so young.

Four years ago, Steven got a runny nose. His family doctor gave him a prescription, but the runny nose didn't go away. A few months later, Steven's vision grew blurry. Linda urged him to go to Wills Eye Hospital. Soon he was getting X-rays and MRIs and talking to an oncologist, David Mintzer.

Steven had a rare, hard-to-diagnose tumor, right behind his nose. When Mintzer looked at Steven's MRI and chest X-rays, he realized the cancer had already spread and would probably kill him. Chemotherapy worked for a year, and then the cancer became resistant. They continued to try new chemotherapies, and also to give radiation to relieve pain and control the tumor's growth. The tumor was growing through his palate.

Last winter, Mintzer faced the hardest decision for a cancer doctor: deciding when to stop treatment.

"On one hand, you're the doctor, and you want to provide hope," he said. "On the other hand, you can inflict a great amount of harm. There's a great potential to cause even more pain with pointless treatments."

Mintzer explained to Steven and Linda that he thought more treatments had slim or no chance of helping, but if they wanted to try, he would. They wanted to keep trying. It wasn't until several months later, in May, that they decided to stop.

Mintzer found more lumps on Steven's chest and side. Chemo wasn't helping. He asked Steven what he wanted to do.

"I don't want any more treatment, since it's not helping," Steven said. "I just want to go home and rest until the time comes."

Steven hadn't heard of hospice. After Mintzer explained it, he agreed to the care. Afterward, the couple and their son drove to a drug store, and Linda went inside for a prescription. Steven held up three fingers.

"What's that mean?" asked the son.

"That's how much longer I have to live—three months."

Young Steven started to cry.

"I'm sorry," comforted the father. "I'm sorry."

"You put up a good fight, and you have nothing to be sorry for," said the son.

"I'm proud of you," said the father.

STEVEN TOLD MARYANNE all that in her first few visits. She quickly realized she must confront two important issues.

One, she had to deal with the resentment Steven had for his family doctor, who had treated him for a runny nose. The doctor had not spoken to him since that day, even though Steven, an HMO member, had to get a referral from him for every cancer treatment.

"He didn't even say I'm sorry," Steven wept one afternoon, convinced that an earlier diagnosis of the tumor might have made a difference.

There was no way for Maryanne to know whether that was true. Nor did it really matter now. What mattered was that Steven talk about his feelings and deal with them, and that Maryanne listen.

"I appreciate your honesty and sincerity," Steven said to Maryanne one afternoon, after pouring all this out. "Just be honest with me. That's what people in my situation need."

Maryanne also knew she had to persuade Steven to talk to Gretchen. "It's not just telling her—it's helping her," Maryanne told him. "We really don't know how much time you have."

Steven told Gretchen the truth in early June, just a few days after Gretchen's son, Donald, was born. Gretchen was stunned. A few days later, Maryanne brought the two together for a long talk. Steven was in bed, and Gretchen sat on the edge.

Steven told his daughter he was worried about her. She had no direction in her life, no goals. He felt guilty that he wouldn't be around to guide her, to help her raise her expectations. Gretchen said she wished her father had told her sooner that he was dying. She would have spent more time with him. She didn't want to be a disappointment.

Gretchen promised she would get a driver's license and return for her GED at Temple University in the fall.

"I want you to seal this with a kiss," Steven said.

Gretchen leaned over and kissed her dad.

THE NURSES PLACED A HOSPITAL BED in the living room, and Steven would be at the center of life in this house until his death. His seven siblings would visit day and night. Linda rarely left his side. When his 18-month-old granddaughter woke up from a nap on the couch, she'd toddle over and plant a big kiss on Steven.

Steven bonded almost instantly with nurse John Sapovits, who came every other day. John asked the most personal questions, but he never embarrassed Steven. The afternoon of Tuesday, June 18, was typical.

"How you feeling today?" John asked.

"OK."

"You look good. How's your pain, Steve?"

"Good."

"On a scale of one to ten?"

"Four to five."

"Move bowels today?"

"No."

"When did you go last?"

"Saturday. Sunday."

John turned to Linda. "How many suppositories do you have left?"

Linda checked the refrigerator. "Eight."

"Great," said John. "If he doesn't go by tomorrow afternoon, give him one of those."

He turned to Steven. "We don't want you getting clogged up."

"Back atcha," said Steven.

Everyone laughed.

The conversation moved on. Steven began talking about the pain of his radiation treatments, and the nurse disclosed that he, too, had been through radiation for a cancer in his mouth and throat.

"It was the most frightening thing," said Steven. "I fear nothing, but when you're getting treated and you can't feel it, and you can't see it, but then you go home, and it's, 'Oh, my God, what has happened to me?' They burned my taste buds right off my tongue. The side effects are terrible."

"They are," agreed John. "They're wicked."

"They should tell people more," said Steven. "I had no idea I would lose all this weight. I used to be 220. Now look at me."

"I was just like you," said John. "I was 220, and I lost 50 pounds in radiation." John grabbed his ample spare tire. "You can see, I've gained it all back and more."

"I wish I could borrow some."

"I wish I could loan you some."

They laughed.

Steven made a sexual reference. "I used to be like a Rock of Gibraltar," he said. "Now I can't get a flare."

"That's the worst," said John.

"That's from radiation," said Steven. "That's the worst thing a man wants to lose."

"You're right," said John. "It is."

"I understand they do what they had to do," said Steven. "But they should explain things."

"You're right," said John. "They really should."

ON THE WEEKEND OF JUNE 22 and 23, Steven had four seizures. Hospice workers went to his house six times, at all hours. Steven was terrified, not only of the pain, but also of what the seizures represented—that he was dying, that the end would be soon.

At their Monday morning staff meeting on June 24, hospice workers discussed Steven's case. He wasn't ready for death, they agreed. He was scared. They considered giving him heavier doses of drugs to diminish pain and fear and stop the seizures. That would make him less lucid, which was not acceptable. They concluded he needed more emotional support.

The hospice workers were worried that nobody in the family was acknowledging how close death was. He'd lost so much weight. His hands were stone-cold. And they worried that Linda was wearing herself out. "He wants her by the bed at all times," said Nancy, the nurse.

The Rev. James Luckey, the hospice's pastoral-care counselor, decided to visit Steven that afternoon.

EARLY THAT SAME MONDAY MORNING, Steven grabbed his son's arm as he was leaving to go to work. Steven had dreamed during the night about a German shepherd wearing a gold chain.

"I want a German shepherd puppy," Steven demanded. "Bring one home."

Steven suffered in the knowledge that drug dealers worked his street, and that he was powerless to evict them. He was failing as a man. He wanted his son to become a man, not so much to take his place but to feel this sense of duty, to protect and provide.

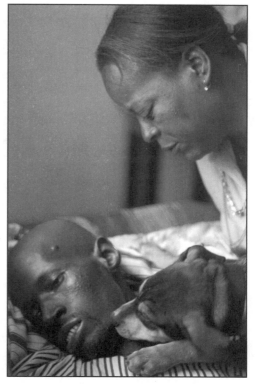

Linda Hendricks allows the new puppy in for a visit; Steven's son had gotten him at Steven's request.

As Steven pulled up that afternoon, in his father's car, Gretchen looked out the window. "There's no dog," she said. Her father, lying in his bed, was confident.

"Oh, yes, there is."

Gretchen looked again. "Ain't no dog."

She kept looking through the window.

"Oh, my God!" she said.

Young Steven walked in carrying a black-and-brown German shepherd puppy and a paper bag with dog treats and toys. He put the puppy down, and off it scampered.

Steven lifted his head off the pillow and watched the pup. He smiled broadly.

"It took seven stores, but I got him," young Steven said. That made his father even happier.

Minutes later, the pastor, Mr. Luckey, arrived. Sitting on the edge of the bed, close to Steven, the puppy nibbling at his cuffs, he asked about the seizures.

Tears streaked down Steven's cheeks, onto his pillow. "I've been shot [as a teenager]," he said, "but there's no pain to describe what those seizures did."

"Steve," said Mr. Luckey, "sounds to me like it should be in the category of suffering, don't you think?"

"I pray every night and every morning. But Jesus won't have me."

The pastor drew closer. He had not expected a confession today. "Is there anything in your life that separates you from the Lord?" Mr. Luckey asked.

"Yes."

"If you don't mind, Steve, I will hear your confession."

Linda sat next to his bed, stroking his arm. Tearfully, almost inaudibly, Steven told a story of how the woman he loved—Linda, the woman he's lived with for 15 years, who cleans his bedpan; his best friend; his heart and soul; the mother of two of his children—is not his wife.

Steven was married to another woman. He had never divorced the other woman nor given Linda his surname. For that, he will never be right with her, never be right with Jesus. He was worried that his legal wife, with whom he had had two children, would receive his life insurance and savings. All that, he told the pastor, would keep him from feeling peace on Earth, from entering heaven.

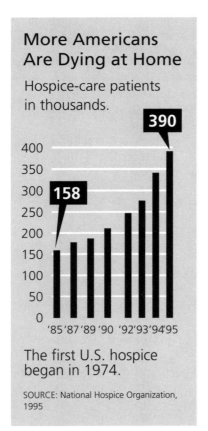

More Americans Are Dying at Home

Hospice-care patients in thousands.

390

158

'85 '87 '89 '90 '92 '93 '94 '95

The first U.S. hospice began in 1974.

SOURCE: National Hospice Organization, 1995

Linda was stunned. "I never knew it bothered you so much," she said.

"It bothered me a lot. It was wrong. You've been a good woman always, but I haven't been a good man."

"Sounds like you want to do right by me, but God doesn't hold that against you," said Linda.

"I agree with Linda," said the pastor.

Steven shook his head in disagreement.

"If I forgive you," said Linda, "then God says it's forgiven."

Suddenly the living room was filled with light. The sun had fallen low enough in the sky so that its rays streamed through the blinds onto Steven, his bed, Linda, the puppy, and the pastor.

"I've heard those things that burden you," said the pastor, "that weigh you down spiritually. I'd like to offer a prayer. Linda has forgiven you. God has forgiven you. That drops it. We all miss the mark of perfection, Steve, and God understands."

"Let us all join hands," he said. "Thank you, God, for our lives, all the good things you have bestowed on each of us, good friends, that special loved one. I just ask you now, Lord, that you restore pardon and peace in Steve's heart. I just ask, Lord, that you could soothe and calm his troubled spirit. I ask that you continue to give him vision—you the great ophthalmologist that can restore the sight to the blind. Lord, I entrust Steve to your care. I just ask you to be with him and comfort him."

There was a moment of silence. The room darkened again. Maybe from a passing cloud.

"Above all, buddy," said the pastor, "I wish you peace."

Steven seemed relieved, almost back to his cocky, confident self. "I know you do, Rev," he said. "You bring out the best in me."

"I'm glad you allowed me to be here," said Mr. Luckey.

"You take the place of my grandma and my ma," said Steven. "You're the shoulder I lean on."

"Those are big shoes to fill."

It was nearly 6 p.m. Mr. Luckey had seen other patients that day. He stood, put on his jacket, and headed home to his wife and his chicken dinner. Steven rolled on his side, and handed the dog a plastic-sausage chew toy. The dog inspected it for a few seconds, snatched it and disappeared under the bed.

HOSPICE WORKERS say they need more time to build relationships and trust, to solve problems, to help dying people accept their fate.

John Mahoney, head of the National Hospice Organization, says doctors should refer patients to hospice earlier than they do. Patients on average

A self-portrait of Steven Jacobs. He took the picture with an instant camera on his 40th birthday, September 28, 1995.

die within 30 to 60 days after hospice is brought in. Fifteen percent live less than a week after starting hospice care.

"If you think about dying as being more than a medical event, . . . if you think about dying beyond that, then there is a role for hospice care earlier on," Mahoney said.

But many doctors are reluctant to refer patients earlier, because they don't want to admit defeat or because they find it difficult to deal with the family's grief. And there's another problem. Enrollment in hospice requires a physician to say that the patient has less than six months to live, but doctors aren't good at predicting this.

About 80 percent of hospice patients have cancer, and their time left is easier to predict. Steven's oncologist, for instance, thought he had three months to live. But many more people in America die from heart disease, stroke, lung disease, and other chronic illnesses, and many of them are not eligible for hospice, in part because their doctors don't know how soon death will come.

"We need to completely restructure our health-care system for people at the end," says Joanne Lynn, director of the Center to Improve Care of the Dying at George Washington University. Lynn says it should be easier to get hospice-like services and more difficult to get useless medical intervention.

Savings from surgery and stays in intensive-care units, Lynn says, could pay for expanded hospice, which costs about $100 per day. Medicare and most private insurers pay for hospice care. Steven's hospice costs, which would total $3,000, were picked up by his hospice, which until recently relied on fund-raising to provide free care.

"Economics is going to push hospice ahead, regardless," said Christine Kriebel, director of the hospice program at Pennsylvania Hospital. "But I don't want to see insurers pushing people into hospice like lemmings over a cliff. I don't think hospice should be the only option. But it should be one option."

STEVEN WAS A DIFFERENT MAN the morning after his confession. His breathing had become irregular. He was foggy, disoriented, drifting in and out. He couldn't eat. Even drinking the nutrition supplement Ensure was too much for him. Maryanne realized he had entered the phase that hospice workers call active dying. This was the end.

Linda couldn't believe it. He had seemed so alive the night before. "I think on Monday night he made peace," she said. "After that, he was ready to go."

He grew worse on Wednesday. When John arrived, he drew Linda into the kitchen. "His breathing has changed," the nurse said. "His liver is starting to enlarge from the tumor, and his diaphragm, which he uses to breathe, can't become fully enlarged. He's more confused, because of decreased oxygen to his brain. His urine will decrease. His appetite will decrease. He could die tomorrow. He could die in a week."

Linda didn't flinch. "He knows he's dying," Linda said. "I know he's dying." After he dies, she said, "then I can break down and cry."

Together they walked back to Steven.

Slurred, drugged, dying, he still knew right away what to ask. "What'd you tell her? You better tell me."

John repeated what he'd told her, that Steven had stopped eating and his breathing had changed. "These changes signal you're actively dying." Steven fought back the only way he could. "Give - me - an - Ensure," he said.

THE NEXT DAY, THURSDAY, JUNE 27, a lawyer went to the house. Maryanne had given Linda a number for the Philadelphia Bar Association referral service and encouraged Linda to call to establish who would get Steven's worldly possessions.

That afternoon, on the day he was called, Ira Mazer from Port Richmond walked in, wearing a blue shirt, tie, and black wing tips. He waived all fees.

Steven lay in bed, in red-and-white striped boxers, one tube leading from his liver, another out his boxers. His eyes were half-open.

"I need to establish you're of sound mind," the lawyer explained. "Do you know where you are?" There was a long pause.

"Home."

"Do you know who this is?" He waited.

"Linda."

Linda said it was time for a seizure pill. She put it in Steven's mouth and offered him a drink, which he wouldn't take. "Did you swallow it?" Another wait.

Steven stuck out his tongue and showed Linda, defiantly yet lovingly, that he had.

"I believe you're pretty with it," said the lawyer.

So he began. "Have you thought about who you want to get your stuff?" The lawyer was talking slowly, as if to a child, but Steven was out of it.

"He's talking to you, Steve," prodded Linda. "You going to answer him? Wake up."

"Who do you want to give it to?" repeated the lawyer.

"To Linda," he whispered. He pointed to her.

"Great," said the lawyer. "Do you want anybody else to get anything?" Silence.

"My son, Steven."

"OK. And what does Steven get?"

"My car, my car."

"And what kind of car do you have?"

Long silence. The lawyer realized this was a silly question to ask a dying man. After all, the car was parked right outside. He continued, "And Linda gets everything else?"

"Topaz," said Steven. "'87 Topaz."

"Is there anything else?"

Steven Hendricks learns from his mother, Linda, that his father is dead. He had gone to pick up relatives and missed the moment of death. "I'm sorry," his father had said when it became clear he was dying. "You put up a good fight, and you have nothing to be sorry for," his son replied.

Steven waved the lawyer closer. Barely audibly, he said, "A divorce. . . . Want to get married."

Linda shook her head. "You're too sick, and it takes too long," she said.

"Even an uncontested divorce wouldn't come through for at least two and a half months," said the lawyer. "Money could probably be used better elsewhere."

The lawyer had what he needed. He returned with a will two hours later. Too weak to sign his name, Steven wrote an X.

IN THE EARLY-MORNING HOURS OF FRIDAY, Chris Jacobs, 48, sat next to his brother, Steven, and read him the Psalms. Steven drifted in and out. At 2, Steven woke up. He couldn't drink from a straw anymore. Linda wet his lips and tongue with a green mouth swab. She knelt beside him.

"I'm happy," he told her. "I'm tired."

"You prepared me for this," she said. "You prepared me every step of the way."

Steven winked.

"I'll be all right," she said. Steven and Linda kissed. Brother Chris and sister Nadine hugged him, then young Steven and Gretchen.

Linda went outside and saw a bright star in the night sky. It was a sign. She went back inside. "There's a bright star over this house," she said. "It's not moving. It's your mother coming to take you home."

"I gotta get up," Steven said.

"And go where?" Linda said incredulously. Steven hadn't been out of bed in a week.

"To the couch," he said. "I'm not dying in no hospital bed."

Chris put fresh pajamas on his brother. Nadine put a sheet and blanket on the couch by the window. Then Chris carried Steven like a bride over the threshold, over to the couch, where he drifted off to sleep. Chris continued to read Psalms.

With family members sharing their grief, hospice nurse Nancy Juergens makes funeral arrangements after Steven Jacobs' death.

About 6, Maryanne and John arrived. Young Steven and his mother were sleeping in the hospital bed—her head at one end, his at the other. Chris was asleep in one chair, Nadine in another. Gretchen was upstairs. The cat was sprawled on the wooden floor. The puppy was at a neighbor's.

On the coffee table was a bag of green mouth swabs, a few of them used. Two Bibles, one opened to Mark 15, the other to Psalm 53. A Polaroid camera. A plastic urinal. Toilet paper. An ashtray with butts. Morphine. A Pepsi. Dilantin. Two beer cans.

Maryanne knelt beside Steven. She held his hand, stroked his head, whispered in his ear. "Your family is with you now. That's what you wanted. And we're asking God to help you. You've got one strong woman."

John checked his breathing and vital signs. "Completely nonresponsive," John said. "He's going to die within 24 hours."

Young Steven, awake by then, started sobbing in the hospital bed. Linda comforted him. "Daddy's not going to be suffering anymore. You go ahead and cry. It's good to cry."

Linda Hendricks thanks the Rev. James Luckey for his eulogy at Steven Jacobs' funeral. Mr. Luckey counseled Jacobs, who told him, "You take the place of my grandma and my ma. You're the shoulder I lean on."

John gave Steven a few drops of medicine from a dropper. "This will help you breathe easier," he said.

"You've done a great job, incredible," John told Linda.

The morning progressed. Linda, John and Maryanne sat or knelt next to Steven. "Death is very undramatic," Maryanne said. "Slow. Waiting. I don't know why, but in movies they dramatize death so. But in real life, it's a slow pace. Not big fireworks."

A day later, Saturday morning, Steven opened his eyes. He looked at Linda. She was holding his hand. He squeezed her hand. She told him she loved him.

A few hours later, he stopped breathing.

"Oh, man," Gretchen cried. "He's died."

Linda kissed him. Gretchen kissed him.

The house was filled with family, and more visitors came, including the hospice workers and Steven's wife and other children. The hearse arrived about 4 p.m. Steven had been with hospice for 31 days.

Linda sobbed all afternoon.

THE FUNERAL WAS SUPPOSED TO BE the next Saturday. The night before, at 9:30, Linda called Maryanne in a panic.

The funeral director, who was charging $5,000, was willing to wait for payment, but the cemetery wouldn't cover Steven with one shovel of dirt until Linda had paid in full—$1,250. Linda was $450 short.

Maryanne calmed Linda. "I'll take care of it." She worked out this solution: Linda would give the cash she had to the cemetery director, and the funeral director would write a check for the balance, tacking it onto his own bill, to be paid when the insurance money came in.

Maryanne and John attended the funeral. They sat in the back row. James Luckey gave the eulogy. Steven had wanted that.

After the funeral, out in the bright morning sunlight, Linda seemed more spirited than she had in weeks. She gave Maryanne a big hug. As she climbed into the limo for the ride to the cemetery, she turned to Maryanne one last time.

"Don't forget about me!" she called. "I want to see you!"

"Don't worry," promised Maryanne. "You will."

EPILOGUE: Maryanne called Linda often and saw her a few times.

Steven and Gretchen were beneficiaries of their father's insurance policy, and each received a small sum after the funeral bills were paid. Gretchen is sure her father is smiling down on her. She bought a car, learned to drive, and enrolled at Temple.

The dog, Remus, is beloved by all—but still chews everything in sight.

3 Taking care of relatives at home: the burden

IT WAS 5 O'CLOCK IN THE MORNING, and Bob Hicks, 64, was certain that he would find his mother dead. He had been a medic during the Korean War. He knew death. He'd smelled it on his mother the night before.

Bob got out of bed, walked a few steps over to an easy chair, and drank a beer left over from the night before. Tears welled in his eyes.

"What could I have done to give her one more day?" he asked himself. But one more day of what? Lying in bed. Helpless. Unable to walk, eat, or often recognize her own son. At age 87, Amanda Hicks was paralyzed from stroke, demented from Alzheimer's, sustained by a feeding tube. Bob knew she'd be better off dead.

Bob walked down the hall to see his father, who had owned and operated a gas station for 40 years. Now, at age 90, William Hicks weighed 117 pounds. He wore a diaper. A feeding tube was implanted in his stomach.

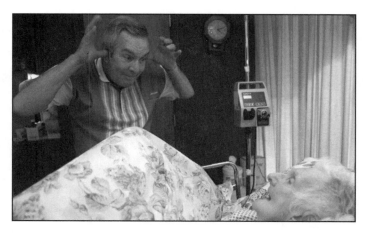

Bob Hicks tries to coax a rare smile from his mother, Amanda. Most of the time she doesn't even know he's her son. With help from home-health workers, Hicks takes care of his mother, 87, and father, Bill, 90, at their home in Haddonfield, N.J.

The light was on in his father's room. Bob poked his head in the door. "Good morning, Dad."

"Morning, Bob."

Saying the two words took nearly all of the old man's strength.

Bob went back into his room, smoked a cigarette, and then went downstairs to the kitchen, where he put on a pot of coffee. He'd need a strong cup. Whatever he found in his mother's room, he'd still have his father to care for.

MODERN MEDICINE can give Americans longer lives but it can't promise good health. Millions of Americans like Bill and Amanda Hicks will endure long, slow declines, and increasingly this will occur at home.

"This is going to be the future of America and health care," said Jeffrey R. Friedman, the primary-care doctor for Bob Hicks and his parents.

Seven million Americans today take care of an ailing or chronically ill parent or spouse at home. The fastest-growing category of Medicare costs is home-health care. And the fastest-growing job category in America is home-health aide.

Care that was once limited to hospitals and nursing homes—feeding tubes, IV drips, catheters, even ventilators—is now being given at home, partly to reduce health-care costs and partly because Americans want to remain at home as long as possible.

The burden of providing this care has fallen on families—on people like Bob Hicks, assisted by an army of home-health workers. New support services crop up almost daily—adult day care, respite care, shared housing. But, ultimately, family members themselves must shoulder most of the physical and financial weight. Most important, they must carry the emotional strain of trying to decide what's the right thing to do, and wondering how they can endure.

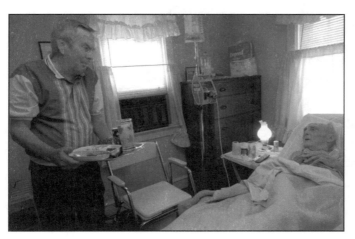

Bob Hicks spends a moment with his dad, Bill. Hicks takes care of both his parents at home. He is among 7 million Americans caring for a parent or spouse at home. Bill Hicks, who ran his own gas station for 40 years, has heart disease and emphysema.

AS BOB MADE COFFEE that morning, birds chirped outside. Bob had grown up in this three-bedroom white house with green awnings on a shady street in Haddonfield, N.J. He moved back after a divorce in the mid-1970s and started an accounting practice, which he sold four years ago, partly to care for his parents.

Growing up, he and his brother, Bill, and his parents once had known all the neighbors. Even until a couple of years ago, his father handed out flags to children for the July Fourth parade. The Hickses now are unknown to many on their street, with no exterior signs of life other than home-health aides coming and going, frequent ambulances, the trash and recycling set out on Fridays.

As the coffee brewed, Bob sat in his living room easy chair, where he spends much of his day. He smoked a Marlboro Light, then another, stacking the butts like tombstones in the ashtray at his side. The coffee was ready, but Bob waited to drink it.

He walked through the kitchen and into his mother's bedroom. Flipping on the light, he looked closely at his mother, lying in bed. Her eyes were open, a blank look on her face. Her foggy blue eyes looked through him, into the middle distance, as if he weren't there.

She was breathing. Amanda had been like that for three years.

"Good morning," Bob said cheerfully. "How ya feeling?"

"Tired," she said.

"You cold? . . . You need a blanket?"

No answer. She kept looking through him.

He kissed her on the cheek. Then he walked out and drank his coffee. Bob didn't care that it was a beautiful day in May. For him, it was the start of another day like all the rest.

MEDICARE HAS SPENT more than $307,000 to care for Bill and Amanda Hicks in the last decade. Much of that, which includes nursing care at home, was spent in the last two years.

Amanda was hospitalized 20 times during the last three years, usually for bladder infections. That cost Medicare $52,817. Bill's hospital bills were higher. Medicare paid $134,250 for 14 hospitalizations. Bill Hicks has also incurred more than 200 bills from a myriad of doctors, labs and other providers in the last two years. That came to almost $30,000. Amanda has nearly as much, for $17,000.

Most days, America pays for two hours of care by a home-health aide for Amanda and Bill—$72 each. Bob pays $400 to $500 a week for additional aides. And then there's Gillian Reeve, a nurse who visits Amanda three times a week, usually for an hour. Reeve is British, and Bob adores her. Just hearing her royal English voice lifts his spirits.

Reeve is competent and caring. Medicare reimburses her employer $89 for each visit.

The price tag of home care for Medicare jumped from $2 billion in 1988 to $15.9 billion last year, and now it accounts for 13 percent of all Medicare costs.

BILL HICKS STARTED SMOKING filterless Camels at age 13. He suffers from heart disease, emphysema, clogged blood vessels in his legs, and other illnesses.

While Bill was in the hospital last December for stomach problems, doctors detected an aortic aneurysm, concluded it was life-threatening, and operated. He spent 50 days in the hospital, nine of them in intensive care. He wasted away to 107 pounds, and lost the strength to feed himself. Surgeons implanted the feeding tube. By May, he was up to 117.

Feeding his father and mother is Bob Hicks' most important job in life. He does it the same way every day. First he does his father. He pours six eight-ounce cans of Ensure Plus, a rich nutritional supplement, into a plastic bag, hangs it from a pole, connects the bag and tubing to the tube in his father's stomach, and turns on the pump for the day.

Bill feels nothing, tastes nothing. The flavor is vanilla.

Then Bob moves on to his mother. "Good morning, Mama," he says. "How are you?"

He knows before he asks what she will say: "Tired."

Bob holds her hand a moment, pulls back the covers, and checks her out— no bed sores. He gives her medicine—a squirt through the feeding tube into her stomach. He takes her pulse, blood pressure and temperature.

The cases of Ensure are stacked against the bedroom wall, as if in a warehouse, an ominous sign of endless days of tube feedings that he must give. Bob hooks her up just as he did his father.

He usually offers his mother a drink of water. He gets a small paper cup, holds a towel under her chin, and gives her a sip. She gags and burps and seems as if she's going to choke. Ever since her stroke three years earlier, she's been unable to swallow, which is why she needs the feeding tube. He wipes her chin, tucks her back in, turns off the light, and walks into the kitchen, where he pours another cup of coffee, adding amaretto-flavored cream.

Bob is proud of the level of care he is providing his parents. Bob took his mother home from a nursing home in August 1995, convinced that he could provide better care, and for much less than the $65,000 a year being paid from his parents' savings. He was right. He just never anticipated that his father's health would plummet, too, and he'd have them both so sick.

Bob's daughters and his brother, Bill, thought he should put them in a nursing home. Bob knew his parents would rather be at home. He also knew a nursing home would consume their savings in a couple of years. And they'd lose the house. Then where would he live?

EVERY MORNING, Amanda gets some exercise. She moves from the bed to a chair. An aide slides a tarp beneath her, then hooks each corner of the tarp to four chains hanging from a hydraulic lift—much like a tow truck driver putting the hook and chains under a car.

Then the aide gently jacks Amanda up, wheels her across the floor—suspended in air like a stork's bundle—and lowers her gently into the chair.

On the morning of May 20, Amanda slipped out of the harness, crashing onto the floor. Blood poured down her face, dripping onto her pink nightgown, from a gash next to her left eye. The aide screamed for Bob, and he rushed into the room. He cradled her head in his hands. "I'm here, Mom. I'm here."

The aide held a towel to the gash and summoned an ambulance with the portable phone. "I want to lay down," mumbled Amanda.

"You are laying down, Mom," Bob said tenderly.

Amanda was hospitalized at Kennedy in Cherry Hill. The Haddonfield volunteer ambulance squad has taken Amanda or her husband to the hospital 30 times in the last 20 months. Bob didn't go. He said he couldn't. The aide would be leaving soon, and who would watch his father?

Bob also said he didn't need to go. He'd spent a year in hospital waiting rooms.

That afternoon, Amanda was back in her bed, with stitches over her eye and a shiner.

Bill Hicks, upstairs, never knew she had been gone.

THE FIRST WEEK of June, Amanda was hospitalized with a urinary-tract infection. Bob went to visit. His mother's room was the last one down the hall. He walked in and was momentarily confused. There were three hospital beds, and in each one lay an old, white-haired woman. IV lines ran in and out of each one.

Amanda Hicks chaperones a prom in the 1940s. Bill Hicks is flanked by sons Bill (left) and Bob, in 1952. Together, the couple have been hospitalized 30 times in the last 20 months.

Bob walked up to the first bed. "No, wait, this isn't her." He looked at the second bed. "There she is."

He walked over, and gingerly and gently, lovingly, he stroked her hair and leaned over. "Hi," he said.

"Hi," she responded.

"Do you know who I am?"

"My son."

Bob was surprised. She hadn't recognized him for weeks. But that did not change Bob's belief that his mother would rather be dead. He often debated whether he should allow her to die. But he believed that removing her feeding tube would be murder and that it would cause a painful, suffering death.

So every morning he wished he would find her dead. But also dreaded it.

Years ago, he said, he asked God to just let her die. But, he said, "God must have been taking a coffee break."

"How ya feeling?" Bob asked his mother.

"Tired."

He stroked her again and left.

Driving home, he thought about the visit. He couldn't believe that he didn't recognize his mother at first.

BILL HICKS KNOWS he's a burden to Bob, but he wants to live. He thinks he has a 50-50 chance of getting better, though "the doctors don't tell you anything."

He agreed to talk about this on a gorgeous June day, tucked in bed, as usual, under his blue blanket. He'd eaten an omelette that morning, and had just finished watching *The Price Is Right.*

He said he never considered how much treatment he would want at the end of his life, or how far his son should go to keep him alive. He said he had never discussed the subject with Bob. Bill Hicks said he believes in God but not in a hereafter. He prays, "but I feel like it's praying to a stone wall." He doesn't like the feeding tube, but he doesn't want to be taken off it if it means he will die.

As for Amanda, he thought his wife would be "better off dead than she is living." He thought she would want to be taken off the tube and allowed to die, though "I just couldn't do it," he said.

What he misses most about being stuck in bed is being out in the yard. "I want to cut the grass, and edge, and plant my tomatoes, my flowers. I'd like to trim the bushes."

His big hope is to "get up, get washed good, go downstairs and cook Bob a good meal: roast lamb, creamed onions, yams."

Asked how he would rate his life on a scale of one to ten, he said: "A seven."

BY THE YEAR 2003, 75 PERCENT of the federal budget will be devoted to Social Security, Medicare, Medicaid, and debt service at current growth rates. That leaves 25 percent for everything else.

Medicare is expected to go bankrupt in five years, 2001, unless Congress acts. And that's before the first baby boomer retires.

Today, the cost of caring for each Medicare beneficiary is shared by 3.9 workers, who pay into the Medicare trust fund. By 2030, the cost will be shared by only 2.2 workers because of all the boomers.

To save Medicare, a number of options have emerged, including raising payroll taxes, cutting Medicare benefits, reducing payments to doctors and hospitals. Such choices are easy in comparison with the next questions:

Should taxpayers pay to repair an aneurysm in a sick 90-year-old man? Should taxpayers buy Ensure Plus and routinely pay for hospital care for an 87-year-old woman who can't swallow and rarely recognizes her son?

To control costs, rationing "is inevitable," said Daniel Callahan, president of the Hastings Center in Briarcliff Manor, N.Y., and a prominent medical ethicist. He believes the elderly must be valued, but at the same time, he said, resources are limited and as a nation, we will have to set fair and compassionate standards.

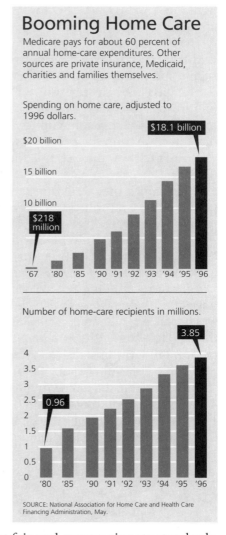

Booming Home Care

Medicare pays for about 60 percent of annual home-care expenditures. Other sources are private insurance, Medicaid, charities and families themselves.

Spending on home care, adjusted to 1996 dollars.

$18.1 billion

$218 million

'67 '80 '85 '90 '91 '92 '93 '94 '95 '96

Number of home-care recipients in millions.

3.85

0.96

'80 '85 '90 '91 '92 '93 '94 '95 '96

SOURCE: National Association for Home Care and Health Care Financing Administration, May.

"Medicare should establish some real priority system," he said, "setting an annual budget and forcing everybody to live within that budget."

Marilyn Moon, one of five trustees of the Hospital Insurance Trust Fund, which finances Medicare, disagrees with Callahan. She said the nation can solve its Medicare crisis—short-term and long-term—without rationing if everyone shoulders the burden equally. As she sees it, nothing in and of itself will be too painful: benefits cut modestly, taxes raised modestly, beneficiaries' contributions increased modestly, payments to providers reduced modestly.

She believes there is no need to panic if Congress and the nation heed the trustees' request for "prompt, effective and decisive action."

BOB HICKS HAD WAITED for Father's Day as a tonic, an elixir. Finally, it arrived.

His two daughters, Brynn and Julie, flew in from Tennessee and Texas. He hadn't seen Julie in three years, Brynn since February. Bob paid for their flights and put them up in a Cherry Hill motel.

The girls were an injection of life. The smell of perfume, the sight of hairbrushes, the peals of sisterly laughter. That Friday night they cooked pork chops—taking some up to their grandfather—and then Bob and his daughters went up the street for water ice.

"I can't tell you the last time there was laughter in this house," Bob told his girls.

After dinner, they went up to their grandfather's bedroom, where Brynn played guitar and Julie sang. Brynn sat on the bed and played three contemporary gospel songs.

Saturday came and went, like a soldier's one-day furlough between Iwo Jima and Guadalcanal. They spent much of the day sitting around, gabbing. Brynn talked of having a baby.

On Sunday morning, Bob's older brother, Bill, drove up from Annapolis. Bill stayed for nearly five hours. First he and his nieces went to see Amanda, who was hospitalized for an infection, and stayed 10 minutes. She didn't recognize them. Back home, they prepared the prime rib, creamed onions, baked potato. Bill went upstairs to invite his dad to join the family downstairs.

"I can't," his father said. "I'm too weak."

They feasted in the dining room. Bob ate so much and laughed so hard that it seemed this meal would sustain him for months, physically and emotionally. The man who hadn't had a day off in two years made plans to meet his brother in Baltimore for an Orioles game and to eat some Boog Powell barbecue.

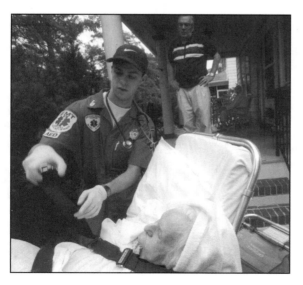

An emergency medical technician takes Amanda Hicks to the hospital. Bob Hicks, watching from the porch, would stay home to be with his father.

After dinner, Bob, his brother, and the girls sat in the living room and talked about Amanda.

"I think it's a travesty to have her sustained like this," said Bob's brother. "It would definitely be a blessing to have her pass away as soon as possible."

"If she were younger," said Brynn, "and there were a chance she would get better, we would say, 'Wait.' But she's lived her life. Her life is over."

"She loved life," continued Bill. "She loved living. I have such wonderful memories of my mother. I loved her dearly. But there is no future. The point is, it's over."

Bob leaned forward in his green easy chair, and looked squarely at his big brother. "Should Mom live or die?"

"I would pull the plug," said Bill.

"Could you do it yourself?" Bob asked.

"Got to be done," said Bill.

"You got brass ones," said Bob.

Brynn and Julie wanted to put their grandparents into nursing homes. "You can't give up your life," said Brynn.

A few minutes later, Bill went upstairs to say good-bye to his father, who was watching the U.S. Open Golf Tournament. Bill was off to North Carolina to visit his own daughter and grandchildren. After all, it was his Father's Day, too.

"I've got to go, Dad. I'll be back soon. In a couple weeks."

"That's what you said the last time. You were gone for months."

"Something came up, Dad. I had to take a business trip. I'll stop back."

"I wish you could help Bob out more."

"I do too, Dad."

A quick hug, and he was out the door. An hour later, Brynn and Julie had to go, too. They had planes to catch.

Bob walked the girls outside into the bright sunlight. Brynn put her guitar into the car trunk. Bob's eyes became misty. They hugged.

"It was great seeing you two," he said.

He stood on the step of the porch and watched their car pull away, leaving him alone on his lonely frontier. He walked back inside, sat down in his easy chair, and sobbed.

ON JULY 8, A MONDAY, at 9:45 a.m., Bob drove two blocks to his family doctors' office. He had an appointment with Joel P. Chack, Friedman's partner. Bob had been wearing a heart monitor for two weeks.

Chack explained that the right side of Bob's heart was wearing out trying to push blood into his lungs damaged from emphysema. The effort had enlarged his heart, and it was now beating irregularly.

"These are all a consequence of your lung disease," Chack said.

"So we have to go to no-smoking again?" Bob said.

Dr. Joel P. Chack delivers some bad news to Bob Hicks about his own health. The doctor prescribed medicines for problems detected after Hicks wore a heart monitor for two weeks. "These are all a consequence of your lung disease," Chack told Hicks.

"That would be a good idea, wouldn't it?" agreed the doctor. "Unfortunately, the horse is already out of the barn." It was a conversation they had had before.

"What can be done?" asked Bob, "and what is the long-term prognosis? Should I go home tonight and start planning the funeral?"

"No, you're not going to be pushing up daisies," said the doctor. "You're serious enough that we hauled your bottom in here. But not serious enough that we throw you into the hospital." The doctor prescribed a number of medications.

Bob wanted to know whether to blame his caregiving responsibilities for his condition.

"What's happening with you is kind of the natural consequences of your smoking," the doctor said. "Now it doesn't help you that you're under a lot of pressure. You've got all that on top of you, and you've got to deal emotionally with the fact that your retirement is turning into a nightmare."

Bob agreed with the doctor's assessment.

"They're both going to be around a while," the doctor added. "They're not going anywhere."

Bob asked for more Valium to help him sleep. He got it. When Bob got home, he smoked a Marlboro Light and started lining up the butts again.

JULY 10, THE MORNING after the baseball All-Star game, was a remarkable day. Cool and beautiful, the summer morning sounds and smells and breezes came pouring through the screen of the open door.

And Kathleen Myall, 47, an $8-an-hour home-care worker for a private home-health agency, arrived to do her magic.

Some aides are excellent. Others sit and watch soaps. Often the house has a revolving door. A few days, or a few weeks, and a new aide.

Myall was the best. An agency paid her wages, but she worked for the Lord, and she would tell you God Himself sent her to the home of Bill, Bob and Amanda Hicks, for they were in desperate need.

On her second day with Bill, she took him downstairs. With his arm draped around her neck, she carried him like a wounded soldier. Bill looked like a new man sitting in his living-room chair. He hadn't done that since 1995.

Today she had even more ambitious plans for him. She was taking him outside. For a walk.

Out went Bill with his walker, in his bedroom slippers and pajamas, Myall right behind, prodding him with her encouragement.

"Wonderful, Dad," she said. "Doing great . . . beautiful."

Bill's longtime neighbor was putting an addition on the house next door. Bill wanted to see it. Myall and the neighbors helped him up the steps. Bill looked astonished. Stunned. He was sitting in his neighbor's new kitchen, drinking a glass of water, his old self, the putterer.

"Beautiful, Jim," he said. "Big refrigerator!"

"Should we go back home?" Myall asked.

"Can I see the rest of it?" Bill asked. Bill got the grand tour.

TWO WEEKS LATER, Bill looked sick and scared as he lay back in bed. Bob thought his dad was acting, to get attention. The frail elderly often try to manipulate caregivers. And the caregivers tend to resent it.

This morning, however, after hearing a rale in his father's chest, Bob called 911.

Pneumonia.

A week later, with his father still in the hospital, Bob dialed 911 again. Amanda was gasping. She had a high fever.

When the ambulance came, he escorted his mother outside and stood in the driveway as they loaded her into the back. "Is this your wife?" a paramedic asked.

"You're lucky I don't deck you," Bob said.

Around 1 p.m. the next day, on Aug. 4, Bob went to see his parents. He walked up to the front desk at Kennedy Memorial Hospital. "I've got a doubleheader today," Bob said, "both my mother and father."

He knew the woman behind the counter, from having gone to the hospital so often. Amanda was in 204, Bill in 213. He walked into his mother's room. She was alone, neatly tucked under a white sheet. He leaned over and whispered, "Hi! Hi, girl." Not even a groan, a stir.

Tears welled in Bob's eyes. Knowing exactly what he will find never prepares him. He took her hand and held it. Then he went to see his dad.

"You look good," said Bob. "A lot better than a few days ago."

"I don't feel so good," said Bill.

"You know you've got a friend down the hall?" Bob asked.

"Yeah," said Bill. He quickly changed the subject. "How you doing, Bob?"

"You didn't watch the Olympics? I ran the 100-meter race—in my car."

They chatted a while, and then Bob went home. Inside the empty house, he retreated to his den and put on a video documentary about World War II, his passion.

Bob had the night off. He stayed home and enjoyed an empty house.

BILL HICKS CONTINUED to gain weight, and by August 30 he weighed 137 pounds. He was back home again, and Bob joked that his father had jowls and a pot belly. Earlier that morning Myall had served him pancakes and sausage, and Bill had forked down every bite.

Bill sat in his living room chair, scanning the newspaper, looking content. For weeks now he had been diaper-free, though he still could not walk more than a few steps and probably never would again.

Bill had watched the President's acceptance speech at the Democratic Convention the night before. The Hickses are bedrock Republicans. "I like Clinton," said Bill. "I think he's done a good job."

Bob looked over from his chair. "Will wonders never cease?" he said.

THE DOORBELL RANG on Halloween night. Bob Hicks climbed out of his green chair and lumbered over to the door, muttering about how "this is the worst day of the year."

Bob opened the door and handed Snickers to the little ballerina and Batman. Bob doesn't really hate Halloween. But he was miserable. Both his parents were in the hospital.

That morning, blood had come through his father's feeding tube. In the afternoon, Bob's father said something he'd never said before: "Bob, I just want you to know I tried to be a good father to you. There's a lot I would have done differently, but I tried my best."

Bob thought that meant good-bye. Nearly three weeks later, his father was still in the hospital.

Amanda was also in the hospital on Halloween night. Her foot had become infected, and doctors wanted to amputate part of it to save her life. Bob wept. "After all she's been through, this poor woman won't even go to her grave whole."

Bob had choices. He could have the foot removed. Or, as his doctor told him, he could take Amanda home and let infection kill her. Bob decided to go ahead with the surgery. He's glad he did.

"They say she can come home in a couple weeks. She'll probably outlive us all."

4 Deciding to die with a doctor's help

JANET GOOD ITCHED AND SCRATCHED until she was bloody. She went to her family doctor, then to a dermatologist, and finally to an internist. The internist talked with her for a few minutes, looked in her eyes, ears and throat, and studied her yellowed skin. He had seen this before.

"I have bad news," he said. "I don't want to tell you until I confirm it with tests."

The following day, Janet Good, 72, a short woman with rose-rimmed glasses who lives in the Detroit suburb of Farmington Hills, Mich., returned to the doctor's office.

"Give it to me straight," she told him.

"You will die," he said.

A giant tumor in her pancreas had spread to her liver and was blocking the flow of bile. It was backing up into her skin, causing her to itch. That was the day Janet Good knew she would die: August 18, 1995.

Janet Good has supported Jack Kevorkian in several assisted suicides, including one in her family room.

She didn't panic or get depressed. Her reaction was matter-of-fact. For 20 years this grandmother of six and great-grandmother of four had fought to legalize physician-assisted suicide. She had always known she would end her life rather than suffer a lingering, horrible death. She had helped many others die. Now, her own time was approaching.

One question remained: Would she commit suicide peacefully at home, far from the media spotlight? Or would she die with the help of her friend, ally and hero: Jack Kevorkian?

ALMOST NO ISSUE has hurled itself into front and center of American public debate faster than physician-assisted suicide. And no one is more responsible for putting it there than Jack Kevorkian, the retired Michigan pathologist who has helped at least 45 people die since 1990.

Former Surgeon General C. Everett Koop calls Kevorkian a "serial killer." Other critics label him out of control, a madman.

Still, many Americans are becoming more accepting of physician-assisted suicide. They want more control over how and when they die. They want an alternative to a painful, protracted death.

In 1982, 46 percent of Americans in a Louis Harris survey supported the right of a terminally ill person to suicide with a physician's help. By 1995, the figure had climbed to 73 percent. And in 1994, Oregon became the only state to legalize physician-assisted suicide.

Janet Good sees Kevorkian as a visionary. She has become his associate and advance team.

Need to reach Kevorkian? Call Janet. Need a date for a suicide? She'll help arrange it. A hotel while you wait? She'll help find it.

She lives in a red-brick ranch house in the suburbs with white shutters and red maples out front. She's been married 54 years to a retired Detroit police inspector. She drives a Cadillac, goes to Mass, votes Republican.

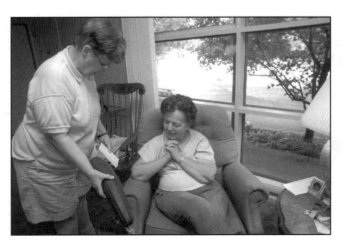

Janet Good with her sister, Margaret Moran, at her home in Farmington Hills, Mich. Good said her ideas about assisted suicide were formed when their mother lived in a vegetative state—"three and a half years of agony"—before dying.

Assisted Suicide - Where the States Stand

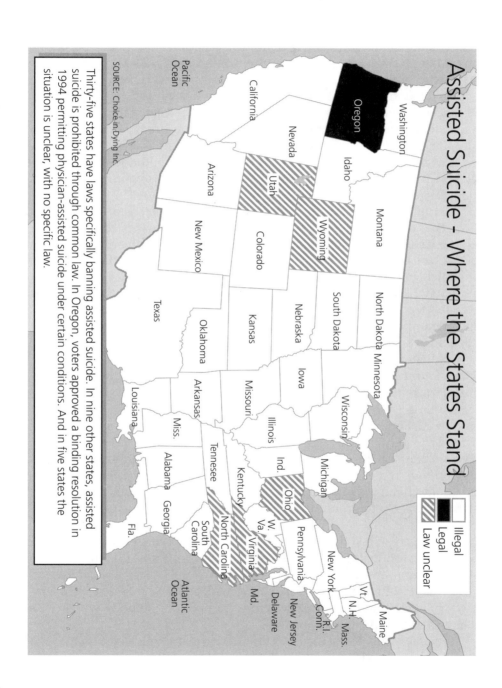

Legend:
- Illegal
- Legal
- Law unclear

Pacific Ocean

Atlantic Ocean

SOURCE: Choice in Dying Inc.

Thirty-five states have laws specifically banning assisted suicide. In nine other states, assisted suicide is prohibited through common law. In Oregon, voters approved a binding resolution in 1994 permitting physician-assisted suicide under certain conditions. And in five states the situation is unclear, with no specific law.

Janet Good became an advocate for doctor-assisted suicide after the night in 1971 when her 83-year-old mother fell off the front porch at home in Detroit and crushed her skull. "My mother ended up in a persistent vegetative state with a huge bed sore the size of a platter on her spine, eating her alive," Janet recalled. "It took three and a half years of agony for my mother to die."

She pleaded with doctors to help her mother die, she said, but they refused.

Janet's mother couldn't get out of bed, couldn't recognize anyone, couldn't speak. Countless times Janet went to the nursing home with mashed-up sleeping pills, determined to put them in her mother's milk shake.

"I would stand there and I would cry, . . . but I could not kill my mother," Janet said. "I have never gotten over the guilt of not putting her out of her suffering."

In 1980, Janet Good founded Michigan's chapter of the Hemlock Society, a national organization devoted to legalizing assisted suicide and euthanasia. She saw this as an extension of her commitment to women's rights. For many years, she was a state equal-opportunity officer and is in the Michigan Women's Hall of Fame.

When Kevorkian surfaced, Janet befriended him. He wanted his first assisted suicide to be at her home, but her husband objected. Instead, Kevorkian helped his first patient, Janet Adkins, an Oregon woman with Alzheimer's, die in his rusty old van in 1990.

Gradually Janet and Jack became close. He'd bring her pineapple cake. Janet found him courageous and kind. Though his flamboyance sometimes frustrated her, she knew he was her ticket to political action.

"I can get what I want for this society by working with him," she explained. She realized that she, too, might want his help some day.

TWO WEEKS AFTER she learned she was dying, Janet underwent a 10-hour operation to remove the cancerous portion of her pancreas. She had rejected chemotherapy or radiation but agreed to surgery, mainly to halt the itching. Doctors told her this would give her six months to live—a year at best.

The surgery wiped her out. So did the painkillers she received afterward. She was delusional. She ripped out the tubes in her nose and throat so doctors had to restrain her arms.

As she lay in her hospital bed, Jack Kevorkian came to see her. This created quite a stir. Only the week before, he had left the body of a suicide client in the hospital's parking lot.

He politely stopped at the front desk, and a guard followed him through the hospital. His visit was social. Janet wasn't ready to die.

"It's not as if I'm eager to end my life," she said later. "But I don't want to die the way I've seen so many people die. . . . Pain management is not the big issue. It's the indignity of having to be diapered and sedated.

People can endure pain. But once their children have to wipe their butts, that's the end. When that dignity is gone, no one wants to live."

As she slowly regained her strength that fall, Janet decided that when the time came, she would die with Kevorkian's help. She had never asked him but knew she could count on him. Death with Kevorkian would be the ultimate political statement, an activist's dream, a death for the cause.

She later reconsidered. On December 19, her husband, Ray Good, had a heart attack and required triple-bypass heart surgery. Janet was sure the heart attack came from worrying about her.

Ray returned home Christmas Eve. That was the worst night of their lives. Donna Unger, the middle of their three children, had planned a party at her home. Believing this would be the family's last Christmas together, she had spent months making a video of Ray and Janet's life together. They had been together since Ray was 15, Janet 12, when they rode bikes on Detroit's east side. Christmas Day would be their 54th wedding anniversary.

As she was wrapping presents that night, Donna Unger keeled over dead from a heart attack at age 51. Janet believed the stress of her own illness contributed to her daughter's death.

Janet began to question the idea of killing herself with Kevorkian. How could she put her family through more upheaval? Wouldn't it be better to die privately at home?

But fighting for assisted suicide had become the most important issue in her life.

SINCE THE 1976 New Jersey Supreme Court allowed Karen Ann Quinlan's family to remove her ventilator, refusing and withdrawing medical treatment have become routine.

Turning off a machine is considered a passive action—without it the patient would die anyway. But going the next step to active intervention—having a doctor prescribe a lethal dose or help with an injection—is a crime in 44 states.

In 1996, however, two federal appeals courts—the Ninth Circuit in California, and the Second Circuit in New York—ruled that terminally ill Americans have a constitutional right to end their lives with a doctor's help. The California court said that Americans have a constitutional right to make sound medical decisions, which include removal of a feeding tube. A dying person's decision to have a doctor hasten his death is just an extension of that right, the court reasoned.

"We see no ethical or constitutionally cognizable difference between a doctor's pulling the plug on a respirator and his prescribing drugs which will permit a terminally ill patient to end his own life," the court wrote.

The New York court cited a different reason: You can't give people on life support the option to end their lives, by removing machines, and not give the same option to terminally ill people who are not on machines.

Supporters rejoiced. Critics attacked.

"No court decision can deny what is fundamentally and naturally true: that assisting in suicide is nothing less than taking another person's life," Cardinal Anthony J. Bevilacqua said. "I ask all people of good will to join me in praying that our society will soon return to support for life and turn away from the culture of death."

The Supreme Court in June 1997 rejected these arguments and kicked it back to the states to wrestle with. "Throughout the nation, Americans are engaged in an earnest and profound debate about the morality, legality, and practicality of physician-assisted suicide," Chief Justice Rehnquist wrote for the Court. "Our holding permits this debate to continue as it should in a democratic society."

ON MAY 6, A GORGEOUS Michigan morning, Janet Good got dressed up in her pink sweat suit—the one with little bunnies pushing a baby carriage on the front—and sat in the front row of a Pontiac courtroom. She attended every one of Kevorkian's trials, always sitting in the front row.

This was Kevorkian's third trial, this time for helping Marjorie Wantz and Sherry Miller kill themselves in 1991. He was particularly brazen, buoyant, indignant that day in court.

Referring to Wantz, Kevorkian's lawyer, Geoffrey Fieger, asked: "Doesn't society have a right to make her suffer?"

"In practice, yes," Kevorkian replied. "In theory, no."

"Do we control our bodies?"

"Not in our society."

"Why do you help the patients?"

"I empathize with patients. I want a physician who says, 'I'll help you.' That's the kind of doctor I want. That's the kind of doctor I want to be. A physician should do all he can to preserve the health and life of a patient, within bounds of patient autonomy. That's one duty. The other part is to arrest and alleviate suffering."

"Why should a physician help people leave this world?"

"That is part of the duty of reducing suffering."

"Isn't it the job of the medical profession to keep her alive even though it's against her will?"

"No."

"Doesn't she have a right to say enough?"

"That is autonomy," Kevorkian said.

During the lunch break, in the courtroom cafeteria, a class of eighth-graders mobbed him, asking for his autograph. "If you had stomach cancer," said one girl, "you'd think he was a hero, too."

AFTER SPENDING THE DAY at Kevorkian's trial, Janet Good held a special event at her house that evening.

A suicide.

Austin Bastable, 53, who lived across the Detroit River in Windsor, Ontario, had suffered from multiple sclerosis for 26 years. His wife and children washed him, dressed him, fed him. He tried to kill himself in 1994, but his wife found him and called for an ambulance.

For years he pushed unsuccessfully for legal suicide in Canada. Bastable's Web page on the Internet—part of a site known as DeathNET—featured video pictures of himself and music from John Lennon's 1971 song "Imagine." Bastable communicated via e-mail, pecking out letters with his left hand. His last entry was dated May 1, the eve of a television interview. "If they don't know how tedious my days are," he wrote, "they soon will. I guess they'll cut out the graphic bits—like my getting an enema while bent over the bathtub."

A day later, a man named Paul Flynn e-mailed a response: "I have MS. I do not want to die. For God's sake, stand up like a man, and stop pretending that quitting is brave. I think you are either a coward or a dramatist, probably the latter."

Through e-mail, Bastable contacted Janet Good and made a date with Kevorkian. Janet had agreed with Kevorkian's request to have the suicide at her home. Ray Good had changed his mind.

After six years of his wife's working with Kevorkian, after six years of hearing her talk with those suffering people on the phone, after getting to know Austin Bastable and his wife personally, after realizing his own wife might soon be in similar agony, Ray Good not only agreed to let Bastable die in his family room, but also built a wheelchair ramp so Bastable could get from the driveway into the house.

When Janet returned from court that evening, Bastable and his wife, Nina, were there. Kevorkian arrived around 8. Bastable was having trouble

Jack Kevorkian and Janet Good, who attends all his trials, meet during a Michigan court break. The pleas for help arrive at her home by letter, phone and e-mail. "We're so busy," she said. "Why can't there be a Dr. Kevorkian in every state?"

swallowing and knew that a feeding tube was next. He had left instructions with the funeral director: "Put a big smile on my face."

As Janet described the scene, everybody assembled in the family room. Bastable sat in his wheelchair, beneath a print of Shakespeare's home, Stratford-upon-Avon, and near a shelf of Reader's Digest condensed novels.

As Kevorkian and other doctors he had invited repeatedly asked if he understood what he was about to do, Bastable blurted: "Let's get the show on the road."

Ray Good shook his hand and said a cop's farewell: "Good-bye. Nice knowing ya." Then he left the room. Janet and her daughter, Marjorie, stayed, with everyone else. Someone slipped a mask over Bastable's mouth and nose, and Bastable turned a metal knob releasing deadly carbon monoxide gas. He also pulled a string, allowing an injection of barbiturates and deadly drugs to flow into his veins, Marjorie recalled.

Janet watched as his eyes closed, his breathing slowed, and he died.

Even though this fate could soon be her own, she thought only of the death she had witnessed. "It was so peaceful, so beautiful," Janet said. "I felt so relieved for him. His suffering was over."

JANET GOOD WAS HAVING a conversation in her living room one June afternoon when the phone rang. She wasn't going to answer it, but the caller identification box flashed her doctor's number.

"Oh, hi," she said sweetly. ". . . Oh yes! OK. OK. Great. Wonderful. I'll probably come by today or tomorrow." She smiled and hung up.

"He prescribed me the pills I want—with refills!"

She could now get enough pills to kill herself and avoid embarrassment. How would it look if Kevorkian's chief lieutenant couldn't get enough drugs to end her own life? She had given too many pills away, helped too many others, and hadn't saved enough for herself.

Janet was so excited she asked her daughter to videotape her picking up the drugs at the pharmacy.

Now she had control. She could take her life when she wanted. She had chronic pain, like a dripping faucet. Her abdomen was bloated. She popped an occasional pain pill, but tried to limit them. They made her foggy, and there was so much to do.

After being acquitted for the third time in May, a week after Bastable's death, Kevorkian and Janet had become busier than ever. In one 10-day stretch, they helped three people die.

ON DAYS WHEN SHE WASN'T helping Kevorkian, Janet and Ray often went gambling. She loved the slots.

On the drive over to Windsor one day in July, Janet revealed something quite surprising. She was embarrassed to still be alive. People had made so much fuss. They'd waited so long—it had been nearly a year since her surgery. Yet here she was, not only gambling, but winning!

"People think I'm a fraud," she said. "Sometimes I feel I should get on with it already."

Inside the casino, Janet relaxed, laughed. She dropped three coins at a time into the slot machines and hit the button. Cherries. Cherries. Come on, cherries! She was playing with the casino's money. She'd won $900 in the last few weeks.

Suddenly, whistles and sirens. Ka-ching, ka-ching, ka-ching! A bar and two wild cherries—480 quarters fell into her happy hands.

Time for lunch.

In the cafeteria, she talked openly about how she might die. She put down her slice of pizza and picked up a spoon. She started mashing imaginary pills in an imaginary bowl. "This is how you do it," she said. "You mash up a whole bunch—I don't want to tell you, but it would depend on your size—you mash them into a powder.

"First you have to eat a late meal, about an hour before. Then you take some seasickness medicine, Dramamine, about half an hour before. This will help you keep it all down. Then you mix the pills with some pudding or applesauce, you need something the right consistency. Then you gulp it down real fast. You want to get it all in before you start to get drowsy or fall asleep. Then that's it. You've done it."

She said her husband wanted her to die in bed next to him. Her daughter, Marjorie, also wanted to be with her when she died, but Janet worried that it could be traumatic for her.

After revealing all that, Janet returned to the slots. Ka-ching. Ka-ching. Ka-ching. Around 3 p.m., she cashed out, down $31.

Back home an hour later, Janet checked her phone messages and mail. "Hello, Janet, my name is Diane . . . I'm calling for help with an assisted suicide. Please call me back." The voice was tragic, pathetic, desperate.

On the table was an overnight-delivery package. Janet ripped it open. Inside were medical records and a handwritten note: "Dear Janet Good, My mother suffers horribly from ALS. She fears going into a nursing home worse than death itself. She is in such misery. Please help us contact Dr. Kevorkian."

"Oh, God, we're so busy," Janet said. "I don't know where we could even fit her in. . . . Why can't there be a Dr. Kevorkian in every state?"

ON SEPTEMBER 6, JANET MET Kevorkian at the Quality Inn in the Detroit suburb of Bloomfield Township. Janet described what happened next.

Isabel Correa, 60, and her husband, Trino Soto, had flown in from Fresno, Calif., and were waiting in a first-floor room. Correa suffered from debilitating nerve disease and spinal-cord tumors. Three months earlier, unable to lift her head, she had undergone surgery to fuse a piece of hip bone into her neck. After that, she decided, no more suffering.

Janet parked her Cadillac on the wrong side of the motel. She walked around and checked on Correa. Janet was the advance team. Her job was to say hello and see that everything was fine. As she approached the room, Janet noticed several people standing around. She saw a man climb down from the cab of an 18-wheeler. Dressed in a suit, he didn't look like a truck driver.

Were these cops? she wondered. Or crazies? She had read about abortion doctors being shot and killed. How did they know she and Jack would be there? Were her phones tapped?

She went into Correa's room and told her they might not be able to help her die today. The woman, sitting in her wheelchair, sobbed. "Please don't abandon me," she pleaded. "Please don't. Is the doctor here?"

Janet told her Kevorkian was waiting in his car. He arrived a few minutes later with his suicide machine and his video camera. He decided to postpone the suicide, but videotaped her plea. He always records his patients on tape before he helps them die, to avoid doubt about his role and their desire.

He had just unzipped the camcorder case, when someone knocked. "Room service."

"I don't want room service," Correa's husband said.

Her muumuu aswirl, Janet Good joins the fun at the luau of her grandson, Jeffrey Unger, in Michigan.

"You want this room service," the voice repeated.

"Oh, no, I don't."

Then another voice: "Jack, we saw you go in there. Open up."

Kevorkian let in the police. No one was arrested, but the police confiscated Kevorkian's video camera and tapes he had made of earlier suicides, including one the authorities didn't know about. Janet got home around midnight.

The next day, in another suburban motel room, Kevorkian and Janet Good helped Isabel Correa die.

MANY OF THE NATION'S leading advocates for improving the care of dying people oppose suicide. They say suicide is a misguided reaction to a medical system that has abandoned dying patients.

"It's a well-documented fact that those asking for assisted suicide almost always change their mind once we have their pain under control," said Kathleen Foley, a pain specialist at Memorial Sloan Kettering Cancer Center in New York and director of the Project on Death in America, an effort to improve care for the dying.

"It is not people in pain but those anticipating pain who most often request physician-assisted suicide," she told an interviewer. "A patient with the support of family and friends, a sense of the transcendent—however defined—and a doctor who makes it clear the patient will not be abandoned is not going to ask to have life ended."

Janet Good contends that suicide must be legalized and medical standards established, precisely to protect people. "Physician-assisted suicide happens every single day in homes and hospitals across America," she said. "And it is not regulated. There is so much room for abuse. People are begging for laws, begging for regulation. The public wants it. Dr. Kevorkian wants it. If we could get this regulated, he would stop."

Critics say doctors have never had the right to take a life, and that giving them such power is dangerous.

"If it came to pass that it was legalized, fine," said Carlos Gomez, a University of Virginia physician who opposes suicide and has testified against Kevorkian. "Find your willing executioners. It's not hard. You can kill in a variety of fashions. We know what drugs to use. Train a group of people, and do it. If it comes to pass, the medical profession should stay as far away from it as possible."

The Clinton administration, through the Justice Department, filed a brief in November 1996 with the Supreme Court opposing assisted suicide.

University of Michigan law professor Yale Kamisar, who has known Janet Good for 20 years and studied suicide laws nearly twice that long, strongly opposes the Supreme Court's legalizing assisted suicide. "We have to take a stand now," Kamisar said. Once the court established that terminally ill people have the right, he said, there would no longer be a legal distinction between withdrawing life support and actively causing death.

Then, he predicts, "there will be 100 lawsuits with people saying, 'I have bad burns,' 'I have a stroke,' and the courts will decide disease by disease, illness by illness, when suicide is permissible and when it isn't. The court will have to balance your interest in ending your life against society's interest in preventing free suicide. Pain is subjective, suffering is subjective," he said. "Where is the thing going to end?"

Arthur Caplan, director of the Center for Bioethics at the University of Pennsylvania, says the issue should be left to state legislatures. "If we see courts trying to carve this out, then we're just lining ourselves up for a reenactment of the abortion debate," he said, "a horrible way to go." Caplan is convinced that several states will eventually legalize suicide.

"We're headed inevitably toward legalization," he said. "I've never doubted it for an instant. A society as obsessed with autonomy and self-determination as we are, as cuckoo over liberty, as fearful as we are of being dependent when we die, as worried as we are about the high cost of dying, and . . . [with] the low status assigned to the elderly in the culture, it doesn't take a sociological genius to predict a movement toward legalization."

And if America legalizes assisted suicide before providing affordable long-term care, Caplan said, old people will feel a responsibility to die, "to end their lives rather than tax the system."

EPILOGUE: In November 1996, police fingerprinted Janet Good and took her mug shot. She was indicted on four felony counts for helping with an August 30 suicide—the suicide police learned about when they seized Kevorkian's videotapes at the Quality Inn.

The judge said he would dismiss the charges against Janet if she proved to him she was terminally ill. Janet has no such intention. She wants no special treatment.

Though she is in constant pain and knocks herself out with narcotics each night, she also doesn't expect to die anytime soon. Janet still has not decided how she will die—with Kevorkian or without him.

Maybe she will just die in her sleep. She says she wouldn't mind that at all.

5 Finding more ways to stay independent longer

ONE MORNING LAST SPRING, Ruth Hilsee, 99, took a stroll to inspect a new apartment. As she clung to her favorite blue walker, the one with four wheels and hand brakes, this 93-pound puff of a woman, bent but ever bubbly, just couldn't imagine moving, even though the staff in her retirement community wanted her to consider it.

She had been living happily in a one-bedroom apartment at Kearsley, in West Philadelphia, for 15 years. She shopped at the Acme, made her bed with more precision than a Marine in boot camp, and kept a checking account, writing $10 checks to charities of every stripe.

Kearsley was opening 60 "personal care" apartments, the trend in elderly living. They were smaller than Mrs. Hilsee's, but offered one crucial advantage: an aide to help daily with dressing, bathing and taking medication—things that Mrs. Hilsee had so far managed quite well on her own.

Mrs. Hilsee toured the cheerful apartment with Alice Evans, a Kearsley staffer. Evans told Mrs. Hilsee she would have space for one lamp, one table, one chair.

For 15 years, Ruth Hilsee enjoyed the freedom of a retirement-community apartment, knowing that help was nearby if she needed it. If she moves from the nursing-home wing, where she's recovering from falls, it will be to the personal-care wing.

In her apartment, Ruth Hilsee, with great-grand-daughter Vanessa Hall, loved having visitors. Below: Mrs. Hilsee, a horticultural-school graduate, in a University of Pennsylvania garden in 1922.

Mrs. Hilsee returned to her apartment. The afternoon sun filled her windows, their sills covered with African violets and many other plants. Mrs. Hilsee graduated from horticultural school in 1918 (she had recently pledged the usual $10!), and when a Kearsley staffer dropped by to ask the Latin name for baby's breath, she replied without hesitation: "Gypsophila." Looking around her apartment, Mrs. Hilsee counted six tables. She thought about the ordeal of moving. What would she have to leave behind? Her books? The oil portrait of her son at age 6? The bedspread crocheted by her mother? Her love seat?

The next day, Mrs. Hilsee wrote Evans a note. She thanked her warmly, but she couldn't possibly move. The day after that, Mrs. Hilsee wrote another note: "Perhaps I should reconsider."

RUTH HILSEE is a success story of modern medicine and social progress: She has lived nearly a century in excellent health, living independently, staying mentally active, finding joy and fulfillment in each day.

Throughout most of human history, half of people have died before their 18th birthday. Today, four of five Americans live to 65. Those who do can expect to live 18 more years.

In just 30 years, America will have more people over 65 than under 18. In 50 years, nearly 90 million Americans will be over 65, and one million to five million could be as old as Ruth Hilsee.

Although Mrs. Hilsee is approaching the end of her life and is content to die, she still has choices to make, and she intends to make them. What she and her generation want most is as much independence as their health will allow.

And America is rushing to comply with those wishes, building personal-care apartments—often known as assisted living—at a rapid pace, to help people like Mrs. Hilsee live in residential settings. To allow them the freedom they want.

AFTER VISITING the personal-care apartment, Mrs. Hilsee spent several weeks discussing the pros and cons of moving with everyone she could find, including her daughter-in-law, Jennie Hilsee, 71, and her three grandchildren, all of whom live in Roxborough.

She discussed it often with her sister, Grace Murphy, just 97, with whom she spoke every night at 9:30. Mrs. Murphy lives at the Quadrangle, a retirement community in Haverford. Mrs. Murphy, who often scolded Mrs. Hilsee for taking a bus to the grocery by herself, encouraged her big sister to move into personal care.

Mrs. Hilsee didn't think she needed extra care, but she was afraid of falling. She had fallen nine years earlier, when she was 90, and had broken her hip. It required six weeks in Kearsley's nursing wing, but she bounced back.

Forty percent of Americans over 65 who fracture a hip die within a year. But Mrs. Hilsee didn't even stop driving. She didn't stop until she was 93, after her son finally convinced her: "He said there were so many wild drivers on the road. And you know they do cut in and all."

The one lasting consequence of her fall was a slight loss of flexibility. Mrs. Hilsee can no longer kneel when she prays. Now she must sit, usually on her love seat. A frequent subject of her prayers is that she will not fall, especially when climbing over the lip of the bathtub, the hardest single physical act in her life. To make bathing easier, Kearsley installed grab bars in Mrs. Hilsee's bathroom and a stool in her tub. But personal care had a walk-in shower! Mrs. Hilsee noticed that feature the moment she toured the apartment.

One morning in May, she decided she needed to know more about personal care so she telephoned Connie Spencer, another Kearsley staffer and dear friend.

Sitting on her perfectly made bed, she put the question to Spencer: "What does personal care mean? Does that mean if you have to go to the dentist, somebody will take you?" Mrs. Hilsee had no intention of going to any dentist. She was extremely proud of her teeth. She had all but one. And she took excellent care of them. She would bite into nothing, cutting up even a tuna melt or tomato sandwich. She thought she had one cavity, but hadn't been to a dentist in years. "They'll probably want to extract a tooth, and that will make me furious," she had said. "I won't have it."

Spencer said rides to the dentist could be arranged, but were not part of personal care. Mrs. Hilsee thanked Spencer and hung up.

"It's such a difficult decision," she said. "I'll just put it in the hands of God."

IN TERMS OF DISTANCE, moving from her apartment to the personal-care wing was not great—from the fifth floor to the first, down a new corridor. But emotionally for Mrs. Hilsee, it would be a leap.

Familiar geography and routine mean so much to the elderly. Mrs. Hilsee loved knowing precisely where everything was in her apartment—from her four magnifying glasses to her three walkers—just as she loved her routine in it.

The morning of May 31 was typical. After washing her face, combing her hair, and hanging her nightgown on the bathroom door, Mrs. Hilsee pulled on her slip and dress, put on her shoes and tied them, and headed into the kitchen to boil water for her coffee. First she took her medicine— two aspirin, two vitamin C, a heart pill and a thyroid pill. She swallowed one pill at a time, each with a sip of her instant coffee, which she cooled with a splash of tap water. Then she had toasted oats, a generic brand. "They're much cheaper than Cheerios and just as good," she said. She carefully opened the bag, untied the twist, poured some into a bowl, and got a milk carton out of the refrigerator.

Mrs. Hilsee prepares breakfast and lunch in her apartment, but eats dinner with other residents in the Kearsley cafeteria. Each night at dinner, she gets a half-pint of milk and takes it back to her apartment for her cereal the next morning.

Opening milk cartons is an adventure. She doesn't have the strength to do what any schoolchild can: push the sides of the carton back, then squeeze them together. This morning she got a sharp kitchen knife and dug into the mouth of the container. Finally, she carved a hole big enough to pour milk into her cereal and coffee. Sitting happily on her kitchen stool, she ate her toasted oats, spoonful after spoonful, down to the last oat, without spilling a drop.

"My, they're delicious," she said, putting the bowl in the sink and rinsing it.

Then she made her bed. It took her 14 minutes, going from one side of the bed to the other, again and again, pulling up the sheet and bedspread, smoothing out wrinkles, punching her pillows. Putting on her wristwatch took five minutes. Fastening the band challenged her dexterity.

Then, as she does every morning, Mrs. Hilsee read a verse in her religious day book. This morning it was Romans 12:2: "And be not conformed to this world: but be ye transformed by the renewing of your mind. . . ." Afterward, as usual, she wrote the citation on her desk calendar.

The two most important dates in her calendar are those of the hairdresser's and podiatrist's visits. She records them months in advance—every third Thursday for the hairdresser, and every sixth Tuesday for the podiatrist. Her hair is thin, short and snowy gray. It doesn't grow anymore, she says, so she never has it cut. The hairdresser washes, brushes, and curls it. Once in a while, Mrs. Hilsee gets a perm, but she can't remember the last one.

Ruth Hilsee shops for groceries, picking only single bananas because she hasn't the strength to separate bunches. At her retirement home, Kearsley, in West Philadelphia, she would prepare her own breakfast and lunch and eat dinner in the dining hall with other residents.

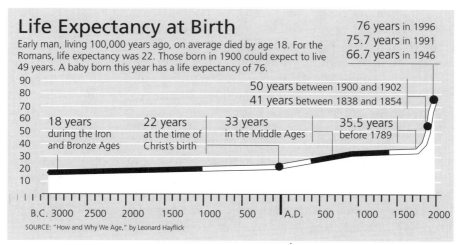

Life Expectancy at Birth

Early man, living 100,000 years ago, on average died by age 18. For the Romans, life expectancy was 22. Those born in 1900 could expect to live 49 years. A baby born this year has a life expectancy of 76.

76 years in 1996
75.7 years in 1991
66.7 years in 1946

50 years between 1900 and 1902
41 years between 1838 and 1854

18 years during the Iron and Bronze Ages

22 years at the time of Christ's birth

33 years in the Middle Ages

35.5 years before 1789

B.C. 3000 2500 2000 1500 1000 500 A.D. 500 1000 1500 2000

SOURCE: "How and Why We Age," by Leonard Hayflick

She always visits the podiatrist when he comes to Kearsley, having her nails cut and her calluses trimmed. Mrs. Hilsee's greatest ailment is her sore feet. The cushioning, the fatty tissue beneath the balls of her feet, has simply worn out. This is common with old people.

As usual, Mrs. Hilsee ate lunch alone, tomato and mayonnaise on bread. She cut the sandwich into small pieces. After lunch she relaxed on her love seat and watched children's shows on public television. She especially loves *Shining Time Station*. Her father worked for the Pennsylvania Railroad, and the show reminds her of him. "Those little engines, their eyes and mouths are so expressive. I try not to miss that one."

She joined other residents in the cafeteria for dinner, carefully cutting up her tuna melt, and returned to her room in time to watch *The NewsHour with Jim Lehrer*. At 7, she switched to Jeopardy! She was joined by a neighbor, Henrietta Peterson. At 9:30, just before going to bed, she called her sister. They chatted a while, reminisced. Every call ends the same way.

"Good night, darling," said Mrs. Murphy.

"Good night, dear," said Mrs. Hilsee.

AS OF 1994, 2.2 MILLION American women, like Mrs. Hilsee, were either unmarried or widowed and surviving entirely on Social Security. Mrs. Hilsee receives $734 a month. For most in her position—and by then, most are women—life can be a struggle. But Mrs. Hilsee lives quite comfortably at Kearsley because its mission is to provide housing to people with low and moderate incomes. Her rent is $231 a month.

In its own way, Kearsley is as pioneering as Mrs. Hilsee. It provides a continuum of care—independent apartments, personal care and a nursing wing—all in one place, and all for low- and moderate-income residents. Kearsley is nonprofit and has combined aggressive fund-raising with tax credits and low-income loans to accomplish its mission. Mrs. Hilsee knows she is quite lucky to live there.

The challenge to America is to provide more places like Kearsley. In Pennsylvania, New Jersey and Delaware, there are about 100 continuing-care retirement communities, often beautiful facilities such as the Quadrangle, where Mrs. Hilsee's sister lives. These places offer all levels of care, but most of them can cost $50,000 or more just to enter. Newer on the landscape are personal-care, or assisted-living, communities. These facilities typically can cost $1,000 to $3,000 a month.

At Kearsley, aside from her modest rent, Mrs. Hilsee must also pay $5.40 for dinner in the cafeteria, as well as for her telephone, groceries, and other personal items. She manages just fine, writing checks and recording each expense in a large ledger, custom-made on graph paper by her grandson. Mrs. Hilsee doesn't trust her arithmetic any longer and allows her daughter-in-law, Jennie Hilsee, to balance her account once a month.

Mrs. Hilsee recently received a windfall—a check from the John Hancock Mutual Life Insurance Co. for $802.63. Mrs. Hilsee's father started the policy with $1 on June 1, 1898. Mrs. Hilsee's parents, and then she herself, contributed a dime a week toward the policy until 1965, when the company stopped collecting nickels and dimes. The account stood idle for 30 years until Jennie Hilsee, sorting through her mother-in-law's papers, noticed a record of it and wrote the company.

Mrs. Hilsee considered getting her love seat reupholstered with the money, but wasn't sure she'd be alive long enough to make the investment worthwhile.

MRS. HILSEE NEVER WOULD HAVE considered moving from her apartment a few years earlier because her best friend, Ethel McHenry, lived next door. Mrs. Hilsee had known Miss McHenry all her life. In 1981, after Mrs. Hilsee's house in Germantown had been burglarized three times, Miss McHenry persuaded her to move into Kearsley with her. She made sure that Mrs. Hilsee got the apartment right next door.

In those early years, Miss McHenry took personal responsibility for Mrs. Hilsee, introducing her and involving her in activities. They were inseparable. But about three years ago, Miss McHenry's diabetes and arthritis and many other ailments began catching up with her, and she moved to Kearsley's nursing wing. In the last year, it was Mrs. Hilsee who became responsible for 95-year-old Miss McHenry. Every night after dinner, Mrs. Hilsee visited her.

"She couldn't hear or see or watch television," Mrs. Hilsee recalled. "We couldn't have a conversation. I used to get hoarse shouting to her. So we would just sit. Sometimes it was a little effort to get down there every night. As soon as I got there, she'd say, 'I'm so glad you're here.' Every night she would be so sad," Mrs. Hilsee continued. "She was just so tired of all her infirmities. She was tired of living. She kept saying, 'I wish I were dead. I wish I were dead.' It wasn't really a matter of suffering as with being bored with life."

Miss McHenry died one afternoon in May while eating lunch. Mrs. Hilsee rejoiced. She knows her dear friend is now happily in heaven, though she does admit she's felt a void since her friend's death.

Mrs. Hilsee believes God keeps her alive for a purpose, and her purpose these last few years had been to comfort Miss McHenry. But now Miss McHenry is gone. Mrs. Hilsee is unclear of her purpose now, though confident God will find her another one. If not, Mrs. Hilsee is perfectly ready to die.

NOT ONLY ARE AMERICANS living longer, but they are enjoying better health. Research by Ken Manton of Duke University, one of the nation's leading demographers, shows that every year a smaller percentage of the elderly suffer from disabilities. Of course, the burgeoning number of older Americans includes millions in declining health. But, according to Manton's research, a smaller percentage of older Americans each year will be sick.

Manton has analyzed the National Long Term Care Surveys, studies of 20,000 Medicare recipients in 1982, 1984, 1989 and again in 1994. His analysis showed that those needing help with daily activities declined from 24.5 percent of elderly Americans in 1982 to 22.6 percent in 1989. He also looked at 16 major illnesses among the elderly, from heart disease to arthritis, and found an 11 percent decrease across the board between 1984 and 1989.

Manton has many explanations: better diet and exercise; fewer smokers; better medicine; common surgeries that help people remain self-sufficient, such as hip replacements and cataract removals. Even simple devices such as grab bars for bathtubs or walkers with hand brakes help older Americans maintain their independence longer.

Though this improves the quality of life, it's the genes that enable people to live as long as Mrs. Hilsee has. That is the conclusion of Thomas Perls, a Harvard geriatrician, who is author of the New England Centenarian Study. The United States has 57,000 centenarians.

"If people have the genetics that is destined to make them die at 70, then they're certainly not going to make it to 99," said Perls. "There are things they can do to get them to 75, whether that is diet or exercise, avoiding smoking and so on. But to get into that old-age, extremely-good-health group, you've got to have those good genes behind you."

Science is hard at work trying to alter the biological time bomb that ticks inside of every cell in the human body. Just recently a conference was held in New York: "Biotechnology: Innovations for Longevity—Living Better as Well as Longer." Dreamers believe that within the next 50 years, science will extend the limit of human life—now considered 120 years—to 150, 200, or 300 years. Many, like Perls, believe that is pure romance.

Perls' research has shown that when people as old as Mrs. Hilsee begin to decline, their health fails swiftly. "You start to have problems in the last year, and then you die," he said.

MRS. HILSEE'S MOTHER died at 85, her father at 66. Her siblings died years ago, except for Mrs. Murphy. Her husband, Donald Ashcroft Hilsee, a retired Philadelphia schoolteacher and Wharton School graduate, died of cancer in 1969, at age 72. Her only son, David, died in 1993 at age 68 from end-stage kidney disease.

Mrs. Hilsee explains her longevity this way: "We were brought up very sensibly, eating things that were good for us, using common sense. That's all."

Yet, she has her limitations. She buys single bananas because she's too weak to pull bunches apart. At dinner in the cafeteria, she gets frustrated. "I can't eavesdrop anymore," she lamented. "People are talking around me, and I can't hear what they say."

Magnifying glasses compensate for weak eyes. She has four magnifiers—in her handbag, by the phone, on top of the *Biblical Archaeological Review*, and on her desk. Still reading is difficult. "I can't look up things in my Bible concordance, and I miss that."

She walked over to her desk and picked up a small, powerful magnifying glass. "Now this one is the best one of all," she said. "And it's so easy to lose it. Jennie found it in the wastebasket once."'

ON JUNE 23, A SUNDAY afternoon, Mrs. Hilsee hosted her grandson Don's 40th birthday party. The group included Jennie, the widow of Mrs. Hilsee's only son; Mrs. Hilsee's three grandchildren, Don, Marietta and Sue; Sue's husband, Fred; and their two daughters.

Mrs. Hilsee was so excited. She made lemonade and had enough trays and chairs for everyone. The visitors brought the birthday cake, ice cream, and soft drinks. Mrs. Hilsee was so pleased that her great-granddaughters preferred her lemonade to soft drinks. The girls, 11 and 9, got a little bored at their great-grandmother's, but they found things to do. They swung on her walker as if it were parallel bars and colored at her desk.

Mrs. Hilsee gave Don a card and a $10 check for his birthday. Don couldn't blow out his candles because they had never been lit. Even the slightest smoke triggers the smoke alarm, which seems appropriate in a building full of old people. As Mrs. Hilsee happily ate her piece of cake, she recounted how, soon after her arrival at Kearsley, somebody burned toast three times, and the fire department came each time. "The last time," she said, "they took the toaster with them."

Mrs. Hilsee reported to her family that she was already planning her 100th birthday party—which, God willing, will be in April. That got her talking about moving. She would never be able to entertain in a personal-care apartment.

"Can you imagine," she told her grandson, Don, "me going to personal care? One lamp. One chair. One table. Why, what would I do without that love seat? I couldn't have Sue and Fred. Where would they sit?"

ON MONDAY, JULY 8, Mrs. Hilsee's next-door neighbor, Henrietta, showed up as usual for *Jeopardy!* But Mrs. Hilsee didn't answer her knocks on the door. She thought Mrs. Hilsee wasn't back from dinner. So she tried again a half-hour later. Still no answer.

Henrietta summoned another neighbor, Marie McAndrew, who banged with her umbrella on Mrs. Hilsee's door. Finally, the two women thought they heard the faintest moaning sounds. They rushed down to the front desk to tell the security guard, who had an extra key. They found Mrs. Hilsee on her bedroom floor. She was coherent but badly bruised. She had fallen. Mrs. Hilsee told the women that she had no recollection of falling. Security called 911.

Mrs. Hilsee spent the night at the hospital. Nothing was broken, and an ambulance returned her to Kearsley, leaving her on her bed, alone, at 7 a.m. About noon, Marie learned from other residents that Mrs. Hilsee had come home. She had kept Mrs. Hilsee's purse and key. Letting herself in, she found Mrs. Hilsee on the floor again.

Again the ambulance was summoned. This time she was admitted to a hospital down the street from Jennie, who spent the afternoon and evening with Mrs. Hilsee. "No broken bones as far as we can tell," said Jennie. "She's badly bruised all over her body. She's conscious and able to answer questions pretty well. She's still upbeat, believe it or not."

Mrs. Hilsee didn't want to return to an empty apartment. "I'm really glad you're going to keep me," she told the nurses.

That night, Mrs. Hilsee's sister called. "I'm so glad to know you're all right," Mrs. Murphy said.

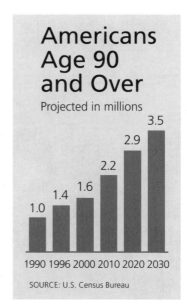

Americans Age 90 and Over

Projected in millions

3.5
2.9
2.2
1.6
1.4
1.0

1990 1996 2000 2010 2020 2030

SOURCE: U.S. Census Bureau

"I can't let you get ahead of me," joked Mrs. Hilsee, a reference to a fall her sister had taken. They talked a little longer.

"Good night, darling," said Mrs. Murphy.

"Good night, dear," said Mrs. Hilsee.

DOCTORS NEVER figured out what caused Mrs. Hilsee to fall. Perhaps she turned her head too far in one direction, cutting off blood to the brain, and she blacked out. After three weeks in the hospital, Mrs. Hilsee returned to Kearsley. But not to her apartment. Nor to the personal-care apartment she had been considering.

Instead she was taken directly to the nursing wing. Her family later emptied her apartment.

Jennie kept the bedspread, hoping that Mrs. Hilsee might use it again one day. Sue and Fred took the oil painting of Mrs. Hilsee's son, as well as the love seat. Mrs. Hilsee found space in her nursing-wing room for the television, an easy chair, her Bible and concordance, and her favorite magnifying glass, as well as several African violets.

AFTER WRESTLING SO HARD with the question of moving out of her apartment, Mrs. Hilsee was surprisingly accepting of the sudden turn of events. In fact, she was relieved. For the first time in her life, she was willing to let others do for her. She was glad to have the safety net.

At 99, Mrs. Hilsee has entered a new phase. She has lost her independence, and that requires an adjustment. But she is improving. She can now dress herself, and when she sees her Bible on a chair across the room, she can get up and get it. Once in a while she is wheeled into the main dining room to eat dinner with her friends.

Though she has come to accept her new life, she has one goal, if only she can get strong enough: She wants to move to the personal-care apartment.

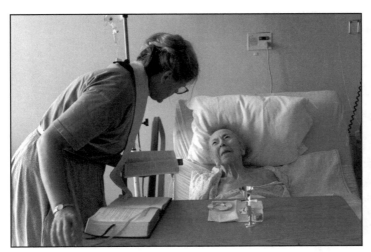

The Rev. Judith Beck, an Episcopal priest, gives Ruth Hilsee communion in her hospital room. Mrs. Hilsee was recovering from falls and afterward moved to the nursing-home wing of her retirement community. At 99, she was adjusting to the loss of her independence.

Epilogue

The effort to improve end-of-life care has progressed significantly since these stories first appeared in the *Philadelphia Inquirer* in November 1996.

More than 70 major national organizations—among them the American Medical Association, the American Association of Retired Persons, American Cancer Society, American Hospital Association, American Nurses Association, Catholic Health Association and B'nai B'rith—have agreed that 10 standards should be established for end-of-life care.

These standards include controlling pain, giving patients and families more autonomy and control over the care they receive, planning end-of-life care in advance, limiting the overuse of high-tech machinery at the end of life, and helping patients feel that their last months and days are meaningful and satisfying.

These groups also have launched a national campaign to make sure the standards are met, and to push for other changes. The effort is called "Last Acts" and is chaired by Rosalynn Carter, wife of the former President.

In other significant developments, the American Board of Internal Medicine has developed guidelines to define appropriate end-of-life care and the AMA has promised to offer continuing-education courses in such care for practicing doctors. Also, the federal government has approved a diagnostic code for "palliative care"—that is, care to moderate pain and suffering. This is a critical development.

Until recently, if doctors and hospitals didn't work on curing or saving a person's life, they could not get reimbursement from Medicare or private insurers—hence they usually wouldn't get paid. Reformers consider recognition of palliative care a major advance.

In 1997, conferences on care for the dying and on the ethics of assisted suicide have been held almost weekly around the country, sponsored by hospitals, medical organizations, religious groups and others.

In short, people are talking—the first, most important step in dealing with dying.

———————————●———————————

Much also has happened to the families I wrote about since their stories first appeared in the *Inquirer* in late 1996.

Patricia Moore and her son, Ron, still live in their 18th-century Pennsylvania farmhouse in Ottsville, Bucks County, slowly fixing it up. Mrs. Moore would like to sell the place and move to Ohio, where she and Gene, her late husband, grew up and where she has relatives. Ron hopes to move there, too, and begin a career as a small contractor, renovating houses.

But Pat Moore continues to grieve and has made little progress improving the house for sale. She misses her husband tremendously and says that virtually every day since his death she has relived his suffering in the intensive care unit. She said she feels awful that he suffered so much in the end.

Mrs. Moore's friend from the intensive care unit, Mrs. Stephano, says her children and friends try hard to keep her from becoming lonely, but she can never predict when sadness will overcome her.

A simple thing like finishing off the mayonnaise in a jar started her weeping. "I realized," she later explained, "that was the last mayonnaise jar we'd ever share."

The family of Steven Jacobs seems to be moving forward. Linda Hendricks, Steven's common-law wife, went back to work a month after his death but then became ill and had to quit. She has returned to work.

Daughter Gretchen lives at home, is raising her two children and taking classes at Temple University to qualify for her high school equivalency, as she promised her father she'd do. Son Steven works at a nursing home.

Books, the cat, one of their two pets, died last fall. But Remus, the puppy, now is a fully grown shepherd and helps to protect the house, as Steven intended.

Maryanne Lohrey, the social worker who was so involved with Steven's care, left the hospice program to enter private practice. She hopes to relocate to New England to be nearer her daughter.

In mid-December 1996, Amanda Hicks died at age 87.

As he always knew he would, her son, Bob, woke up one morning to find his mother dead. After a small service, she was buried in the Baptist Cemetery.

Bill Hicks died on a Saturday afternoon in July. He had been failing quickly, and at times was delirious. His son, Bill, was up visiting from

Maryland. As Bill was leaving that morning, his dad said: "Don't go. This is the last time you'll see me alive."

He was right. Bob was watching his cooking shows on TV that afternoon, checking his dad every 15 minutes. About 4 p.m. he found him dead, his eyes open.

Bill Hicks was never a religious man. The year before his death he said he didn't believe in everlasting life. In his last few weeks, Kathy Myall, his home-care worker, had given him a cross, which he pinned to his pajamas. A treasure, he told her. In the casket the cross was pinned to his tie.

Janet Good died at the end of August 1997, in her suburban Detroit home, after a two-year battle with pancreatic cancer. Until her death, she had been busy with Dr. Kevorkian, helping suffering people end their lives. With local people, she said, the assisted suicides are so secret that police and the media never learn that she and Kevorkian have been involved.

Mrs. Hilsee, who celebrated her 100th birthday on April 22, 1997, lives in a private room in the nursing wing at Kearsley, in many ways the same woman she was before she collapsed in her bedroom. She receives visitors, eats with her friends in the main dining room many days and entertains the family on Valentine's Day and Easter.

She no longer walks, however, getting around instead in a wheelchair. Her eyesight is failing, so that she rarely even watches her beloved children's shows on Channel 12. She faithfully attends weekly religious services at Kearsley.

Mrs. Hilsee tried to tell her family not to make a big fuss over her birthday. They would hear none of that. Her family and Kearsley threw a big shindig.

Even her baby sister, 97, was there.

Appendix

WHERE TO GET INFORMATION

Adult day care

Twenty years ago, America had fewer than 20 adult day-care centers, where the elderly go to socialize or to give their caregivers a break. Now the country has more than 3,000, a number that could double in 10 years. Adult day care receives little support from the federal government or private insurers, but still can be much more affordable than nursing homes ($150 a day) or home health aides ($15 to $20 an hour).

Nationally, call 800-677-1116 for area agencies on aging. Have address, zip code and county of residence handy when calling the Eldercare Locator.

In Philadelphia, contact the Philadelphia Geriatric Center's Weiss Adult Day Health Center at 215-456-2919.

To find out about other adult day-care centers, contact your county agency on aging. In the Philadelphia region:

Philadelphia	215-765-9040
Bucks County, Pa.	215-348-0510
Chester County, Pa.	610-344-6353
Delaware County, Pa.	610-713-2121
Montgomery County, Pa.	610-278-3601
Camden County, N.J.	609-310-8900
Burlington County, N.J.	609-265-5069
Gloucester County, N.J.	609-384-6910

Home care

Home-care aides do everything from cooking and cleaning house to bathing and dressing the patient. Medicare covers limited home-care services for people over 65 who also require skilled nursing care. If paid privately, aides typically cost $15 to $20 an hour. Skilled nursing care can cost $80 to $90 an hour.

Here are some sources for more information:
—Southeastern Pennsylvania Chapter of Alzheimer's Association: 215-925-3220 or 800-559-0404.
—Philadelphia Corporation on Aging, Senior helpline: 215-765-9040. Long-term care: 215-765-6580.
—County Agency on Aging: For 8-county Philadelphia area, see phone numbers above, under "adult day care." Or check the Blue Pages of the phone book for your County Agency on Aging, which provides information on services and facilities for older Americans.
—Pennsylvania Association of Home Health Agencies: 800-382-1211.
—Home Health Assembly of New Jersey: 800-957-4663 (from N.J. only).
—Children of Aging Parents, Levittown, 800-227-7294.
—National Association for Home Care: For area agencies, write Consumer Guide, Box 15241, Washington, D.C. 20003.
—Health Insurance Association of America: 888-844-2782, ask for long-term care insurance guide. Or write: HIAA, Department of Publications, 555 13th St. N.W., Suite 600 East, Washington, D.C. 20004.
—National Association of Professional Geriatric Care Managers: 520-881-8008. Or write: NAPGCM, 1504 N. Country Club Road, Tucson, Ariz. 85716.

Hospice care

Hospice is a movement to allow people to die at home, surrounded by the things and the people they love. Its mission is to support both the dying patient and the family emotionally, while tending to physical needs.

Hospice services include medications, medical equipment, nursing care, counseling, pastoral care, and home-health aides to help with bathing, dressing, cooking and cleaning.

Medicare and many private insurance companies cover the cost of hospice care. To qualify for hospice, patients must have six months or less to live. They must agree to stop seeking medical treatment to cure their illnesses and accept comfort care only.

A list of Philadelphia-area hospices, with addresses and phone numbers, appears below. For additional information, contact the National Hospice Organization at 1901 N. Moore St., Suite 901, Arlington, Va., 22209; telephone 800-658-8898.

AREA HOSPICE CARE

Pennsylvania

Bryn Mawr	Community Health Affiliates Hospice Program	610-526-3265
Chester	Crozer Hospice, Crozer-Chester Med. Ctr.	610-447-6141
Coatesville	Brandywine Home Health Agency Hospice	610-384-4200

Doylestown	Doylestown Hospital Hospice	215-345-2079
Drexel Hill	Delaware County Memorial Hospital Hospice	610-284-0700
Lansdale	Hospice of North Penn VNA	215-855-8297
Lower Gwynedd	Compassionate Care Hospice	215-540-1244
Media	Compassionate Care Hospice	610-892-7741
Norristown	VITAS Healthcare Corp. of Pa.	610-275-2370
	Montgomery Hospital Hospice Program	610-272-1080
	Wissahickon Hospice at Norristown	610-278-2515
	VNA-HHS Hospice Home Care	610-272-1160
Philadelphia	Yedid-Wefesh-Jewish Hospice Chaplaincy	215-790-0444
	Presbyterian Hospice	215-662-8355
	Hospice Program of Pennsylvania Hospital	215-829-7820
	Palliative Care Program Fox Chase Cancer Ctr.	215-728-3011
	Wissahickon Hospice	215-247-0277
	Trinity Hospice	215-351-9000
	Hospice of the VNA of Greater Philadelphia	215-581-2046
	Calcutta House	215-222-1262
	Albert Einstein Medical Center Hospice	215-456-7155
	Holy Redeemer Hospice	215-671-9200
Phoenixville	Community Visiting Nursing Services	610-933-1263
Plymouth Meeting	Samaritan Care Hospice	610-940-1555
	Hospice of the Delaware Valley	610-941-6700
Quakertown	Life Quest Home Care	215-529-6100
Ridley Park	Taylor Hospice	610-595-6000
Sellersville	Grand View Hospital Hospice	215-453-4210
Upland	Crozer Hospice, Crozer-Chester Med. Ctr.	610-447-6141
West Chester	Neighborhood Hospice	610-696-6574
Willow Grove	VNA of Eastern Montgomery County	215-881-5800

New Jersey

Cherry Hill	VITAS Healthcare Corp. of Pa.	609-661-5600
Marlton	Compassionate Care Hospice of N.J.	609-985-0202
Moorestown	Samaritan Hospice	609-778-1339
Ocean View	Trinity Hospice	609-390-9100
Runnemeade	Trinity Hospice	609-939-9000 Ext. 7157
Trenton	Hospice of the VNA of the Delaware Valley	609-695-3461 Ext. 2222
Vineland	Cumberland County Hospice	609-794-1515
	Trinity Hospice	609-691-5666
Camden	Our Lady of Lourdes Medical Center	609-757-3500

LIVING WILLS AND MEDICAL POWERS OF ATTORNEY

A living will is a legal document that allows a person to accept or refuse end-of-life medical care. Some wills are detailed, others more broad.

Living wills have become increasingly popular since 1990, when Congress required hospitals and nursing homes to provide information to patients about living wills upon admission. Living wills were never intended to be used in emergencies, but rather as a guide. Advocates strongly believe that a living will alone is not enough, that families should talk among themselves well before a crisis arises about how much care and treatment an individual would want.

A medical power of attorney is a legal document that allows a person to appoint someone he trusts to be his spokesperson when he can't speak for himself.

For more information on a living will, or for answers to other end-of-life questions, contact Choice in Dying, 200 Varick St., New York, N.Y. 10014, telephone 800-989-9455, fax 212-366-5337.

ORGANIZATIONS

Long-term care

— Pennsylvania Association of Non-Profit Homes for the Aging: Executive Park West, Suite 409, 4720 Old Gettysburg Road, Mechanicsburg, Pa. 17055; 717-763-5724.

— New Jersey Association of Non-Profit Homes for the Aging: 760 Alexander Road, CN1, Princeton, N.J. 08543; 609-452-1161.

— American Association of Homes and Services to the Aging: 800-675-9253.

— Pennsylvania Health Care Association (represents for-profit institutions and services): 2401 Park Drive, Harrisburg, Pa. 17110; 800-990-7206.

Longevity research

— International Longevity Center: Box 1070, Mount Sinai Medical Center, New York, N.Y. 10029; 212-241-1472.

— Alliance for Aging Research: 2021 K Street N.W., Suite 305, Washington, D.C. 20006; 202-293-2856.

— Biotechnical Industry Organization: 1625 K Street N.W., Suite 1100, Washington, D.C. 20006; 202-857-0244.

Assisted suicide

Physician-assisted suicide is illegal in most states. Some organizations that have taken positions pro or con:

— Hemlock Society of the Delaware Valley: 215-963-0069.

—Project on Death in America: 212-887-0150.
—International Anti-Euthanasia Task Force: 614-282-3810.
—Archdiocese of Philadelphia: 215-587-3703.

RESOURCE GUIDES

Advance Directives: Planning for Important Health Care Decisions. Includes forms for "a living will"—medical directives to be followed if you become incapable of indicating your decisions (e.g., "I do/do not want cardiac resuscitation") and for the appointing of a surrogate to make medical treatment decisions for you should you be incompetent. Forms are legally specific to individual states. Forms and instruction booklet available from: Choice in Dying, 200 Varick Street, New York, N.Y. 10014 (212-366-5540); $3.50 (specify state of residence).

Advance Directives for Health Care. Planning Ahead for Important Health Care Decisions. Produced by the New Jersey Commission on Legal and Ethical Problems in the Delivery of Health Care (the New Jersey Bioethics Commission). Booklet contains information and forms for designating in advance your medical treatment preferences; includes three sample advance directive forms and a description of the advantages and disadvantages of each. Contact New Jersey Bioethics Commission, CN 061, Trenton, N.J. 08625.

A Time to Prepare: A Practical Guide for Individuals and Families in Determining One's Wishes for Extraordinary Medical Treatment and Financial Arrangements. Includes forms and instructions for power of attorney, advance medical directives and living wills, organ donations. Edited by Rabbi Richard F. Address, director, UAHC Committee on Older Adults/Committee on Bioethics/Committee on the Synagogue as a Caring Community (New York: UAHC Press, 1994). Address: 838 Fifth Avenue, New York, N.Y. 10021 (212-650-4120); $6.95.

Other resources

—Compassion in Dying, P.O. Box 75295, Seattle, Wa. 98125 (206-624-2775).
—Death with Dignity National Center: 520 South El Camino Real, Suite 710, San Mateo, Cal. 94402 (415-DIGNITY).
—Americans United for Life: 343 South Dearborn, Suite 1804, Chicago, Ill. 60604 (312-786-9494).
—National Right to Life Committee: 419 Seventh Street N.W., Suite 500, Washington, D.C. 20004 (202-828-8800).
—American Medical Association: 515 North State Street, Chicago, Ill. 60610 (312-464-4430).

INTERNET WEB SITES

—Center for Bioethics
  University of Pennsylvania
http://www.med.upenn.edu/bioethics
3401 Market Street, Suite 320
Philadelphia, PA 19104-3308
215-898-7136

—The International
  Anti-Euthanasia Task Force
http://www.iaetf.org/
P. O. Box 760
Steubenville, OH 43952
614-282-3810

—Project on Death in America
  Open Society Institute
http://www.soros.org/osiny.html
888 7th Avenue
New York, NY 10106
212-757-2323

—National Hospice Organization
http://www.nho.org/
1901 N. Moore Street, Suite 901
Arlington, VA 22209

—Answers Magazine For Adult
  Children of Aging Parents
http://www.service.com/answers/
  cover.html
P. O. Box 9889
Birmingham, AL 35220-0889

—Eldercare Web
http://ice.net/kstevens/
  ELDERWEB.HTM

—The U.S. Census Bureau
http://www.census.gov/
Washington, DC 20233
301-457-4100

—U.S. Social Security Administration
http://www.ssa.gov/
1-800-772-1213

—SeniorNet/The International Community
  of Computer-Using Seniors
http://208.215.76.129/
1 Kearny Street, 3rd Floor
San Francisco, CA 94108
415-352-1210

—Pennsylvania Association of Non-
  Profit Homes for the Aging
http://www.panpha.org/
Executive Park West, Suite 409
4720 Old Gettysburg Road
Mechanicsburg, PA 17055-8419
717-763-5724

—Healthcare and Elder Law Programs
  Corporation, a California non-profit
  group
http://www.palosverdes.com/
  helpcorp/index.htm
1611 South Pacific Coast Highway,
  Suite 103
Redondo Beach, CA 90277
310-540-2601

Related resources on the Internet

— The Detroit Free Press' series,
  "The Suicide Machine":
http://www.freep.com/suicide/
  index.htm

— American Association of Homes
  and Services for the Aging:
http://www.aahsa.org/

— Administration on Aging, U.S. Department of Health and Human Services:
http://www.aoa.dhhs.gov/

— The Right to Die Society of Canada,
  DeathNet, advancing what it calls the
  "art and science of dying well." Includes living wills, advance directives,
  links to more information on terminal
  illnesses, literature on suicide:
http://www.islandnet.com/deathnet/